MY MARCH WITH CÉSAR

MY MARCH WITH CÉSAR

Marco E. López-Quezada

A Prickly Pear Publishing Book
1704 Llano St, Ste B-1403, Santa Fe, New Mexico 87505

My March With César by Marco E. López-Quezada
Book design Rolando Hernández Rodríguez Brown

Monterey Sheriff's deputy attempts to serve a court summons to UFW President Cesar Chavez during a large march through downtown Salinas, Calif. Mar. 7, 1979. UFW's general counsel, center, blocks the deputy, left, from serving the subpoena to Chavez, right. (AP Photo/Paul Sakuma)

All inquiries and permissions requests should be addressed to the publisher.
Library of Congress Cataloging-in-Publication
López-Quezada, Marco E.

My March With César / Marco E. López Quezada. — 1st Prickly Pear Publishing ed.
p. cm.
Memoir.
ISBN: 978-1-889568-01-0

Printed in the United States of America
10 9 8 7

PRICKLY PEAR PUBLISHING

New Mexico, California, Texas

Para
María Esperanza

Table of Contents

Introduction

A memoir by its very nature requires one to thoroughly review those events in one's life that are within the ambit of the memoir's focus. It is within that focus that is identified locations and persons who have interacted with the writer and played a part in those events; family members, teachers, partners---personal and "camaradas en la causa"---friend and foe alike. Likewise, a memoirist is compelled to examine these events and select those that carry forward the central story of one's journey. In my case, aside from the first parts which are foundational, the major thrust pertains to my introduction, preparation for, and involvement in the historical UFW farm workers' movement that took place in the 60s through the early 80s.

As a child I was fortunate that my mother, Maria Esperanza, taught me the importance of hard work, respect for one's nation, and, the vital importance and responsibility of fighting for others less fortunate than oneself, the downtrodden or "los de abajo." It was she who first taught me how and when to fight for social justice. My teachers too, religious and lay, were integral in that nascent development. Sisters of Mercy Mathilde and Dolores stand out in grammar school, as do Christian Brothers Gilbert Chatfield and Kenneth Biggs in high school. I am grateful as well to Mary Himmelhoch, my Speech and Debate instructor who encouraged me to go on to law school, and Ramiro Perez, who guided me beyond the class lectures and textbooks to understanding the importance of adopting a geopolitical perspective in analyzing our Chicano reality; a macro to micro approach.

At Garces Memorial High School, it was my classmate Jean Brooks who encouraged me to go to Delano and see for myself what was going on in the farm workers' movement. It was the reason I decided to do my last civics project on the Union, attending the breaking of Cesar's first long fast accompanied by Senator Robert F. Kennedy and thousands of workers assembled at a Delano park. On that day I captured with my Super-8 the historic event and the departing Senator who gave me a shout-out. It was this UFW event that first captured me and provided the "call" that I would eventually answer.

By the time I volunteered to boycott grapes in Los Angeles in 1970, I had decided to get my law degree and return to the UFW as a volunteer attorney. Once having been a Christian Brother at my high school, it was LeRoy Chatfield who took me under his wing in the summer of 1970 in LA, Delano, and Salinas when the Union embarked on organizing the vegetable workers and battling the Teamsters who had signed a sweetheart deal with the growers. It was in that summer too that I met Jerry Cohen, the UFW general counsel. After Cesar and Dolores, these two men were influential in cementing my intention of becoming a lawyer and returning to the UFW.

I thank both Dolores and Cesar for the opportunity they gave me to serve and the trust they extended to me.

As my story unfolds you will read of the many others who helped me along the way, among these were my former wife, Vickie Hernandez, who left a promising television career in the Bay Area to join me in La Paz, taking up a number of exciting projects assigned to her by Cesar. When chosen by Cesar to be the UFW's general counsel it fell on me to organize a new volunteer legal department. I am grateful to Vickie and all the attorneys, paralegals, interns, and clerical staff who answered Cesar's call; a special thanks to my division heads Diana Lyons, Carlos Alcala, and Frank Fernandez. Also, thanks to my *comadre*, Ellen Eggers, who played a key role in the education of four of our paralegal/apprentices who went on to pass the California bar examination on their first attempt, thereby going on to becoming full-fledged and seasoned lawyers; the Hon. Marcos Camacho, Chris Schneider, Ned Dunphy, and Barbara Macri.

Much gratitude goes out to those friends, confidants, and supporters de gueso colorado who throughout my trajectory have always been there for me: Salvador Arriaga, LeRoy Chatfield, Jose Castorena, Esq.,

Jack Brito, Maria Fuentes, David Romero, and grandson John Brody Romero for his encouragement and millennial motivation. Special thanks as well to my friend and lawyer, Sidney Flores.

This writing project has been a truly collaborative project from its inception and credit must first be given to developmental editors Marjorie Rodgers, and, John Pett. I am particularly proud of and thankful to Odilia Galvan Rodriguez of Prickly Pear Publishing, my publisher who has helped me "bring it home," so to speak. Ms. Galvan Rodriguez and I met in Delano in the mid-seventies when we were both volunteers in the UFW. Now, years later, synchronicity has brought us together once again to join efforts on this book. Honorable mention is extended to her editorial staff and cover designer, Rolando Hernandez Rodriguez Brown.

Finally, a special heartfelt thanks to Anna Irene de Barraicua, who during the lengthy writing process remained both my muse and devil's advocate and without whose help this project may have never come to fruition.

Gracias.
MEL-Q
Escondido, California

1.

The sun cast its long shadows about my grandmother's *rancho* in La Norteña, Chihuahua, Mexico. It was the summer of 1958 and I was eight years old. When the night began to fall, the scent of burning pinewood permeated the air, announcing the end of another long day. La Norteña is a small pueblo located in the Sierra Madre Occidental mountain range, which runs north-south on the western border of Chihuahua, adjacent to the Mexican state of Sonora. This mountain range is home to the Tarahumara and Apache nations.

My great-grandfather, Juan Núñez, settled La Norteña in the late nineteenth century. It did not happen overnight or without hardship. He was shot three times by the Apaches and left for dead, but he was smart enough to turn on his stomach and compress his wounds to expel the forming blood clots, according to my maternal grandmother, *abuelita* Domitila Núñez de Quezada. Despite the Apaches seeing him as a "*hijo del diablo*" (son of the devil), he always felt that there was enough room in this big world for everyone. Right or wrong, the fact is that he miraculously survived, and slowly, La Norteña grew to be the small mountain pueblo that it is today.

La Norteña in the late 1950s was very much like living in the United States in the late 1800s. There were no television sets, no electricity, and no running water. Instead, there were wood-burning stoves, horses, kerosene lamps, and outhouses. There were also no telephones in La Norteña.

My brother, Florencio, and I rode the train for ten hours from Juarez, Mexico, which is just across the border from where we lived in El Paso, Texas to La Norteña. The train had a late nineteenth-century coal-burning engine pulled by *Ferrocarriles Noréste de Chihuahua*. When Mom communicated with us from El Paso, she would go to Juarez to a ham radio operator, and from there called us by way of shortwave radio. Our Uncle Edmundo, one of Mom's older brothers, had a shortwave radio in his store in La Norteña and we would go there to speak to her.

When vacationing with *abuelita* at her farm, I did not miss the conveniences of modern life. Once the initial shock subsided, I was very happy amid the simplicity of farm life. Running barefoot, playing in the mud, building wooden trucks, climbing trees, and running from the angry bulls we recklessly provoked added to the thrill that we young boys thrived on.

My brother Florencio and I played with our cousins almost daily. Heriberto Martinez and his younger brother Rubén lived across from our grandmother's cornfield. Back home they would be second cousins, being as they were grandchildren of Aunt Carolina, Mom's oldest sister. In Mexico, we considered ourselves cousins to level the playing field.

At the end of each day, I heard the cooing of doves and pigeons in the distance. They slept above the high roof beams of the barn. The cows, pigs, and horses rustling below settled in for the evening. I looked out the kitchen window and saw my uncles, Miguel and Jorge, securing my grandmother's farm animals. The murmurs of the animals mingled with their hushed voices. That was their nightly routine. One evening, on the last day of our visit, for sure they were discussing the turbulent weather that had passed through La Norteña just hours ago.

Before the storm came it had been a typical day. Early in the morning we did our daily chores about the *rancho*. We ate breakfast and then we went horseback riding with the two Rascón brothers, who were expert riders. We rode up to the small lake at the edge of the pine forest and then galloped back as soon as we noticed the dark rain clouds and strong, cold winds.

When we returned to *abuelita's rancho,* she was at the chicken coop, standing in front of the gate and leaning on her cane, yelling, "*Ooopa, ooopa, ooopa! Ooopa, ooopa, ooopa!*" She hollered until she saw the hens and little chicks racing out of the cornfield with all their chicks trying desperately to keep up. The rooster was right behind them with his head up high, looking alertly to all sides.

Abuelita often used this warning call, but that was when the chicken hawks were circling above her farm. Today, the hawks were nowhere to be seen and her alert was a storm warning!

The chickens rounded the corner of the coop with their chicks running so fast some tumbled out of the pack. Three struggled to get up and a hen ran back to them, making sure they were safe. Once they were all in the coop, I slammed the gate shut.

"Boys, come quickly!" *abuelita* shouted.

"Florencio, Heriberto, go and put the corn cobs in the shed, also the tubs that are in the back!"

The dry corn cobs were kept in large aluminum tubs and had to be put in the *galera.* The danger in handling anything metal during a storm is that it attracts lightning. Florencio and Heriberto knew this, and their eyes were open so wide that with their hair disheveled they looked like "*lunáticos*," as Rubén called them.

"*Si abuelita!*" Florencio called back to her.

"You two, make sure your uncles have put the goats in the barn!" *abuelita* yelled to Rubén and me. My *tíos* had put all the animals in the barn and *tío* Jorge yelled at us to get home quickly.

The wind was so loud I had to strain to hear *abuelita.* She was holding on tight to her shawl and cane, her long black dress and apron blown against her body as she leaned against the wind, struggling not to be blown over. The first thunderclap startled me, then a bright flash of lightning temporarily blinded me. I caught a glimpse of Florencio, who looked very worried. He ran to my side, tugged on my shirt, and pulled me toward the house. As I got to the door it dawned on me that we had left *abuelita* behind, so Heriberto and I ran back to the chicken coop. She was not there. We looked for her everywhere we could think of before returning to the house, all the while dodging small pieces of debris being blown about by the storm.

As we got back to the house, *abuelita* was at the kitchen door yelling for us to get in. To this day I do not know how she got to the house before we did. After we ran in, she tried to shut the door behind us, but was unable to. The force of the wind was too much for her, so we all shoved ourselves up against the door. Florencio managed to secure the iron latch. The heavy door continued being tested by the wind, which pounded against it repeatedly and strained the lock and hinges. We could hear loud slamming noises against the cabin. A large branch from the pine tree just a few feet away shattered the window next to *abuelita's* Singer pedal sewing machine.

Lightning struck all around the cabin. The deafening metallic thunder shook the ground beneath us and resonated deep within me, while the roof of the house was pelted by hailstones. The dirt road out front ran like a rushing, brown river and the gardens inside the yard were flooded to the level of the porch. Three huge branches of the swaying Alamo trees were torn away.

As the storm continued I began feeling enclosed as if I was sitting in a cave. Although I was aware of the intense activities around me, I could no longer hear distinctly, and I was overcome by a feeling of detachment. It emptied me of all fear, and as I sat there next to *abuelita*, listening to all the thunder and pelting rain, I felt safe. With the gradual easing of the storm I could still hear voices but only as if in the distance. I did not register who spoke or what was said, nor did it matter to me. I remained in this peculiar cocoon for what seemed like hours.

That evening, after the storm had passed, we all ate dinner at my grandmother Domitila's house: Florencio, *tia* Carolina, my uncles Edmundo, Mike, and Jorge, Cachira, the maid, and *abuelit*a. Dinner consisted of *frijoles de la olla* (pot beans), chile *colorado*, *quelites* (wild spinach), and handmade flour tortillas, all cooked on the old cast-iron wood stove in the warm light of three kerosene lamps.

After dinner, *tío* Mike told Florencio and me that rather than taking the train north to go home, we would all make the long trip "*al norte*" (north) with Chapo and Colorado (*abuelita's* horses) pulling the wagon loaded with the animals and plenty of *tía* Carolina's pan dulce. When necessary, he added, we would pitch a tent for the night and continue on the next day.

"But *abuelita* can't go," I told him. "She's too old to ride Chapo."

"Sure, she can!" my uncle assured me, explaining how he would tie a blanket between Chapo and Colorado for her to use as a hammock. The fantasy *tío* Mike spun for me was very real and exciting. The thought of going on an adventure from La Norteña leaving no one behind made me happy, making the thought of seeing my mother even sweeter.

Because of the violent storm I had begun to feel homesick, which is, I guess, why he wove the story in the first place. I believed *tío* Mike. As we readied for bed, he played his Tarahumara violin and sang old songs like "*El Caballito Blanco*." I had heard these songs growing up and knew they were the same songs he had played for Mom and her siblings when they were children.

"Prestame tu caballito blanco para echar una carrera por la orilla del barranco..." (Lend me your little white horse to race on the edge of the cliff...)

I lay in bed looking at the dancing figures on the wall and ceiling conjured by the flames of the fireplace. The firewood was crackling, and my thoughts of our wagon pilgrimage north drifted into my dreams. Outside, the cool air and scent of wet earth blended with that of the dark, pine forest nearby. The full moon would soon rise, marking the end of our summer.

But our rustic pilgrimage was not to be. Very early the next morning, Florencio and I were woken by *tía* Carolina, who had started packing for us days ago. Grandmother insisted that we have a hearty breakfast and packed enough food for the long train ride to Juarez and on to El Paso.

During our breakfast, *tío* Mike came in from the barn with fresh milk. It was warm, frothy, and sweet. He gave us a wink, then hugged us both goodbye before leaving to work in the corn and bean fields of Domitila's *ejido.* An *ejido* in México is a plot of land farmed communally under a system subsidized in part by the federal government. *Tío* Mike continued cultivating the land with a horse-drawn plow pulled by Chapo and El Colorado until his death in 1973. It was then that my few remaining relatives moved from La Norteña to the capital, Chihuahua.

After breakfast, *tio* Edmundo came in his Ford pickup to take us to the small *pueblo* of Chico, from where we would take the train on to Juarez. Chico looked just like a western movie set, with only a few small houses and a quaint hotel. Smoke rose from the chimneys and wood-burning stoves. The sun had just peeked above the mountain tops that surrounded the village as we boarded the train.

2.

My parents divorced in 1953 and I did not see much of my father until I was eight. In 1958, after returning to El Paso from our Chihuahua vacation, my brother and I traveled by train to our place of birth, Douglas, Arizona, to stay with Dad for a couple of weeks.

During the two weeks we spent with Dad, my mind often wandered back to El Paso and to my friends at Clardy Elementary, the school I attended through the second grade. I thought of our Mom who two months earlier, while Florencio and I vacationed in Chihuahua, moved to Bakersfield to set up her new business. Therefore, the vacation with Dad was fun, but awkward at the same time. I felt in a strange way disloyal to my mother just for being with his side of the family. I also felt guilty, given the kindness they all extended to my brother and myself. Mom had always been careful not to poison us with the bitterness of their difficult marriage and resulting divorce, but unlike my brother (who was six at the time) I had only been three, which was insufficient time to bond with my father and his family. With my brother it was different. The divorce tore their relationship apart. He had a different set of reasons that made his visit complicated.

I compared the highlights of our two trips. First, our visit with *abuelita* Domitila and Mom's family, especially *tío* Miguel, or "Mike" as they had called him in Dawson, New Mexico when the Quezada men all worked in the mines; the quaintness and excitement of life in La Norteña, our farewell storm. Then our second trip to Arizona when we spent time with Dad's family, our paternal *abuelita*, Amadita, and her loquacious parrot; the dank Bisbee, Arizona mine, rich in copper, labor strife, and history; the sweltering Arizona desert with its white sand dunes, the antiquated gas stations and "The Rattler Museum" with both large and small, dark and colorful, deadly reptiles.

When we left Douglas, my brother felt a deep sadness, one he internalized all his life. He was stoic through and through. Mom believed it was his Yaqui blood. As for me, I was pensive and quiet throughout our two-week stay, and toward the end I was looking forward to our move to California. I felt the three of us—Mom, Florencio, and I—would be just fine.

On August 8, 1958, Dad drove us north on old Highway 99 and down into the San Joaquin Valley over the mountain pass known as "The Grapevine." It was a hot summer day when he dropped us off in Bakersfield, and it was one of the few times I ever saw him.

As Dad had driven through the desert from Arizona to California, I sat in the back seat studying the Chevron map of Arizona. Interstate Highway 666 fascinated me, how it snaked up or down the cross formed by the borders of Arizona, New Mexico, Colorado, and Utah. It uncoiled right at the entrance to Douglas. But my favorite part about the trip was the "World Famous Wagon-Wheel Motel," a western-style motel built with pine log beams, wagon wheel pattern curtains, and cacti, huge cacti everywhere! The Wagon-Wheel Motel marked our halfway point, and Dad got us a large room.

The room's two large lamps were of a hand-carved wooden cactus design, and through the lampshades, made of light brown cowhide, one could see the veins outlined and illuminated by the warm glow of a yellow light bulb. They resembled the Chevron map, but punctuated by several marks from branding irons.

At bedtime, I looked out the window at the desert that surrounded us. The giant saguaros were tall and ominous at first sight. I stared at them, and I focused on those closest to me. I compared their size and shape to each other. The moon cast a soft bluish glow on them.

I focused next on those furthest, those standing behind in the shadows. Indistinguishable and numerous as they were, I became aware of their likeness to those in the forefront. To me they formed a vast, silent army. To my amazement, the more I looked at them the more they took on a human likeness, and before long I saw not cacti, but tall desert warriors standing in formation. Lying on the bunk bed in my cowboy pajamas, I gazed wide-eyed at the saguaro leader who I imagined ready to lead a victorious army. I was awestruck and the fantasy lulled me to sleep.

Our transition to Bakersfield was rapid. By the time I started school there I had discovered certain cultural differences between Texas and California. For one, in El Paso my brother and I were huge fans of a television program called "The Gray Ghost." It was that series, in conjunction with the history lessons taught us in school, which made me partial to the Confederacy--- the only exception being slavery, which Mom and The Catholic Church taught us was sinful. In fact, not only were General Robert E. Lee and the confederate soldiers our heroes in Texas, we actually believed they had won—or, should have won—the Civil War. It did not take me long to adjust. Within a few episodes of watching the "Rin-Tin-Tin" show, I adopted the "blue coats" as my new heroes, and, while the Gray Ghost was relegated to but a fond memory, I was not thereafter an altogether ardent Yankee, either.

From the time I started school a couple of years earlier in El Paso, Mom had clearly expressed to my teachers that they need not tolerate any disobedience on my part, but rather, if necessary, they should not hesitate to spare the rod. For her, a student's good conduct was of utmost importance, and that was the report card grade she always reviewed first. She never missed a school open house and was keen in creating a good rapport, cooperation and trust with our teachers.

When it came time for her corporal punishment spiel I casually walked away.

The only exception to Mom's general rule of disciplinary collaboration came when I was in the second grade. While playing with my friends one day, I was rudely yanked from the playground and taken by my teacher to stand in front of an outside wall. I was instructed to stand about one foot away from it and remain there until she called me into class. I stood there, rather embarrassed at first, but then, imagining different images formed by the stucco. Time passed by very quickly.

This was my punishment for speaking Spanish, my mother tongue. Many years later I would learn that Cesar too was punished for this offense when in grammar school.

Later that day, during dinner, I told Mom about the incident at school. My mother was rather incredulous, and again, because of the importance she placed on our good conduct, she was upset but wanting to verify what I told her. The following day, she took an hour in the morning off from work at Fort Bliss and went with me to school to see my teacher.

While I knew my mother was still upset, I also knew she could keep her cool. She would also stress to us when dealing with others we should do so "*con guantes blancos*," which meant with respect. I actually felt uncomfortable, a bit of a snitch for telling on my teacher.

When we arrived, my mother took me to the principal's office, where both the principal and Miss Thomas were already waiting. Mom shook hands and directly asked the teacher about the day before, whether she had indeed punished me for speaking Spanish. My teacher admitted it and somewhat self-righteously added that if I was to learn English, Mom should speak English to me at home. My mother, on the other hand, responded that there were two reasons she did not speak to us in English: first, she did not feel confident doing so because of her broken English, and secondly, equally importantly she emphasized, in order that we not forget our native tongue. For those reasons, she told Miss Thomas her rule would be that Spanish would remain my primary language at home.

I was proud that my mother had stood her ground and defended me, happy also that a truce was reached. Never again would I have to face another wall. From then on, I was treated very well by my teacher, and from then on too, my mother regularly had Spanish reading and writing assignments waiting for us when my brother and I arrived home from school. By the time we entered high school, we could both read and write Spanish with ease.

"Son, believe me, here you will get the best education" --

I heard her say, as I reluctantly got off the car at Our Lady of Guadalupe and saw her drive away.

This was the school she had chosen for us. She had a knack for this kind of thing, for at times making it sound as if a particular decision was ours instead of hers. I suspected then, and know now, that what she really meant was that at Guadalupe I would get a strict education. No doubt, my rebellious nature worried her.

Growing up I knew that we were not truly a Catholic family, as such, what I did not know was the reason. I found it interesting, however, that although Mom was diligent in having us go through our first Holy Communion and enrolling us in Catholic schools, she rarely ever attended Mass with us. In her defense, that was the one day she could clean our home, spic-and-span. Florencio and I would join her right after attending mass at *Sagrado Corazon* (Sacred Heart), our parish church in El Paso's Barrio Segundo.

Also, there were never any religious statues, crucifixes, or richly colored votive candles in our home as I saw in those of my friends---no rosaries, scapulars, or "holy" water, either. The only thing I did have above my bed was a framed classic print of a guardian angel guiding two small children across a broken ladder-bridge, and a Bible---an illustrated Children's King James Edition.

It wasn't until I was about twelve years old at Our Lady of Guadalupe elementary school that this Catholic family mystery was revealed to me.

Mom told my brother and I that in Chihuahua, Mexico, when my maternal grandmother was but twelve years old, she went to confession at her parish church. Although the story was related to me by my mother, as the youngest and closest to abuelita, she had heard more and assumed the role of the Quezada family historian. Mom continued revealing the secret; of how abuelita entered the confessional, closed the curtain, and knelt down, waiting for the priest to open the screen door and hear her confession. As she waited in the dark booth, she said her prayers to herself while clutching her rosary. Upon hearing the screened door slide open, she began her confession---

"Bendíceme padre, que he pecado..." (Bless me father, for I have sinned)

She strained in vain to hear the priest hidden behind the screen, but there was no quick response or acknowledgement as was normal. Then the priest spoke to her:

"Hija, déjame calentar mis manos en tus pechos." (Daughter, let me warm my hands on your breasts.)

---was the only thing the priest said, asking her whether he could warm his cold hands on her breasts.

Domitila immediately slipped out of the confessional and never again set foot in a Catholic church. This disgrace, perpetrated by a priest against a young girl was repulsive enough, but the fact that it occurred in the intimacy of an enclosed confessional booth, constituted not only a crime, but a gross breach of priestly vows.

After leaving the Church, *abuelita* dedicated herself to studying the Scriptures at home, singing protestant hymns, and always doing good deeds for people. She remains until today, my highest standard of a good Christian.

In my way of thinking, however, there was another reason that I should not have attended a Catholic school.

When I was seven years old, Mom took my brother and I to visit our tía Hortencia, tío Alfonso, and cousins in Mexico City. We toured the Muséo Nacional de Antropología; attended an opera at Bellas Artes at which incoming Presidente Adolfo López Mateos was present; saw the Aztec archeological site of Teotihuacán with its pyramids of the Sun and Moon; walked the hallowed grounds at Castillo de Chapultepec, where in 1847, a young Mexican military cadet, Juan Escútia, wrapped himself with the Mexican flag and jumped from the roof of the castle to keep it from falling into U.S. hands.

But despite all these interesting historic and touristic sites, the one that engraved a more lasting memory for me was the unofficial site, one not found in many tourist books--- "El Muséo de Las momias" (The museum of Mummies).

Before we left Mexico City the summer of 1957, Mom told us that there was this one last site she wanted us to see.

In the 1950s there was much excavation done in the Mexican capital, known also as "el DF," standing for federal district. During the construction of the city's metro rail, infrastructure, and high rises, fantastic archeological sites were discovered which would immediately be announced to the public. Often this aroused a public clamor for preservation and the inevitable temporary halt of construction. The battery of archeologists, anthropologists and cadres of student volunteer excavators would converge on the particular sites to delicately excavate, identify, catalogue, and remove the artifacts to various museums throughout the country.

Associated with these discoveries, there was the inevitable press involvement, notifying the public of the historic findings. In some cases, the excitement pitch was felt not only throughout Mexico, but the entire world at large.

There was one such find, however, that was not publicized. It was one my mother, for some unknown reason, was determined that we see.

The day before we were to return to the United States, we left early from the residential district of San Ángel, where my tíos lived, to find the "Museum of the Mummies." Having only been given general directions to the museum, my Mom asked for the location of what was to be our last touristic site. But all she got were quizzical looks from the local residents.

It should be pointed out that in other parts of Mexico, "*chilangos*" as they're known, are said to be about as courteous as New Yorkers, which is not a compliment. While we did not find this to be the case, on this particular quest, the assessment was proving quite accurate.

In a Catholic country, as is Mexico, the general public does not like to hear of pregnant nuns being plastered alive and pregnant in convent walls—-not casually, at least. But that was the information Mom was going by and she was determined that we see it with our own eyes.

At one point toward the end of our search, Mom saw a building with two soldiers guarding the large doors of a dilapidated, colonial building. We headed directly to them and Mom asked,

"Perdón, es este el muséo de las momias?" (Pardon is this the Museum of Mummies?)

The soldiers looked at each other, then one turned and answered,

"*No señora, las momias aquí están muy vivas.*" (No m'am, the mummies here are very much alive.)

So, Mom had enquired at a jail where as the guard pointed out, the "mummies" were quite alive.

But we did eventually find the *muséo*, and in fact did exhibit mummified nuns, just as Mom had been told. And, some had been pregnant when plastered in basement walls.

The Church's fall from grace in the eyes of my family may have first occurred many years ago in some faraway confessional booth in Mexico, but that morning at Our Lady of Guadalupe I asked myself,

"Why am I here?"

The truth is my third grade would prove to be a difficult one for me.

Mom rented a small house on Beverly Drive, on the east side of town, not far from her new Mexican food business, "La Bonita."

My brother and I were enrolled in Our Lady of Guadalupe elementary school. I was in the third grade and he in the sixth. The small mission school established in 1921 was run by the Sisters of Mercy, and the parish ministered to by the Holy Ghost Fathers, both very old Catholic religious orders.

Mom's business grew fast. She threw herself entirely into it and within a few months secured enough retail customers to begin threatening the competition. With time, Casa Tortillas, that had been established for years before our arrival, succumbed to La Bonita, which overtook it as the label sold in most large and small markets within a thirty-mile radius of Bakersfield. The competition closed its doors and we prospered even more.

We celebrated our first Thanksgiving settled in Bakersfield in 1958 doubly, for Thanksgiving also marked the anniversary of my Mom's return to the United States. Having been born in Dawson, New Mexico, and then taken to Sonora, Mexico by my grandparents, my *abuelito* Agustín made certain to register her as a Mexican citizen "born abroad."

Mom's US birth certificate was in a dainty lady's handkerchief and tied with a pink ribbon when she crossed the US-Mexico border at Douglas, Arizona, at the age of twenty. The immigration officer smiled when he was handed it; then smiled again when he assembled it and handed it back to her, granting her entry. It was Thanksgiving Day, 1945.

Now, in 1958, resettled in Bakersfield and with Mom's Mexican foods business thriving, we had much to be grateful for. Our Thanksgiving Day was shared with the La Bonita employees and their families in our small but brightly decorated home.

The Monday after, as she was accustomed, we forty or so students were each asked by Sister Mary Vincentia whether we had gone to Mass on Thanksgiving Day. I had not gone, and when it came time to answer, I was truthful; I had no reason not to be. I thought.

Hearing my response---all eyes turned to me—as if I had cussed. She pivoted and walked toward me, slowly but deliberately.

"Eloy, stand up."

Her eyes pierced mine. Her stood immediately in front of me, her face ashen and somber. The inquisition continued when I stood.

"Can you tell me, and the class, why you did not attend Mass on Thanksgiving?"

Mentally I rushed through all the Ten Commandments, Baltimore Catholic Catechism book, lessons, and bingo~

"Sister, Thanksgiving is not a Holy Day of Obligation."

The day not being a holy day of obligation I was not required to attend Mass.

All the fury of hell could not be contained in her dark eyes, and you could have heard a pin drop-- were it not for Benny Ramirez.

I heard him cracking up uncontrollably behind me, distracting Sister Vincentia much like a bull is intentionally distracted when a bullfighter is in trouble. Sister Vincentia spun around with flair, and walked away from both of us heathen boys. I knew though that it would not end well between us.

Benny had won the day for me and I was grateful to him. We became friends from that day onward.

The Christmas of 1958, I was given a black, Schwinn 3-speed bicycle, exactly like my brother's. Come spring I too would be able to get to school by riding the three miles distance without Mom having to interrupt her work day which on some days started as early as 4:30 a.m.

I could now also train as an altar boy. This would require that I be up before sunrise and be at the Sisters' of Mercy convent on our school property, before 6:00 a.m.

As I recall during my third-grade year, we had three Holy Ghost priests at Our Lady of Guadalupe church. They lived in the rectory, their home and office, located also on the school grounds, opposite of the convent. They were Fathers Küster, Reilly, and Burkhart, listed oldest to youngest.

In my third grade it was Father Küster who trained the altar boys. He did so by having us assist him, in two-by-twos, with serving the early Mass in the convent that was home to eight nuns. The training took place on weekdays and our training and education in Latin took approximately four weeks to complete.

The priest had a full head of white hair. Despite being German he was of swarthy complexion. His dark eyes were set deep and fixed, with dark circles under them. He rarely smiled. He had told us once in a religion class that he had been in a concentration camp during World War II, though I don't recall why. If he did tell us, I may have been distracted wondering instead why his right small finger was crooked. I often did. In later years I recalled him when I broke the same little finger. I still do when people ask me why mine is crooked.

In any case, his demeanor was stern. I did admire his knowledge and intelligence until in the eighth grade he openly declared himself to be against Darwinism.

"When you go off to college someday and your professor tells you that you evolved from a monkey, you tell him Father Küster sends his grandmother his best regards."

New Years, 1959, passed and by February I had pretty much grown accustomed to my new school. I was happy that I was no longer the new kid on the block. I had my small circle of friends, was doing well academically, and thanks to Ralph Alonzo, was excelling at all the marble games.

One day that spring, without any notice, Father Küster came to our class and asked to speak with Jimmy Malone and me. In his heavy German accent, he gravely told us that we were to report to the convent the following Monday at 6 a.m. sharp, otherwise,

"I'll box your ears off."

I hoped he'd smile, but he didn't. Jimmy and I didn't either. My brother had told me Father Küster often said that to the boys in his class, who were three years ahead of us. He too had been trained by Father Küster and considered it kind of his sense of humor.

I wasn't so sure.

On the very last day of my altar-boy-training by Father Küster, after days of losing sleep, going to school, memorizing the Latin responses that we repeated like parrots, I got up and raced out of the house and three miles to the convent.

I was running late so when I rode into the school yard, I simply dropped my bike and ran in the convent where Jimmy and Father Küster were waiting. I was still half asleep and disheveled.

I quickly put on my cassock and darted into the small chapel as I struggled with the surplice. I knelt to the right of Father Küster, no more than two feet distance away him, as was Jimmy to his left.

The Mass began with a short Latin chant by the sisters and Father Küster, and then began the ritual. At some point prior to the consecration of the host and wine, I was trying to keep up using the laminated cards which we servers were still allowed to use, even though Jimmy and I had it down pat.

I was struggling to stay awake. On top of it, I had not had a chance to eat anything, so I was nauseous as well.

At some point, when Father Küster said "Sanctus," it was my responsibility to ring the altar, or "Sanctus" bell. It calls the attention of the worshipers in attendance to the celebration of the Holy Eucharist.

Father Küster and Jimmy continued droning on in Latin, is all that I recall, when…

BANG!

What startled me awake was a booming sound and stinging pain from Küster's large knuckle---come crashing down on the crown of my head.

I buckled at my knees and even as I tried hard not to fall backward from my kneeling position, all I could see was a blinding light that little by little resolved to a bluish soft sight.

I remained stunned. I knew I had not heard the "Sanctus" before

Küster's blow—but after the blow—I distinctly heard subdued giggling coming from behind me. I looked around and through the bluish haze; I made out two of our young nuns sitting close together with their hands to their mouths. One of them was Sister Mary Vincentia, my Thanksgiving inquisitor.

As soon as it ended, I got out of there like a bat out of hell.

The next week, I was officially enrolled as an altar boy and still have the pin given to me by Küster.

3.

After the third grade, I began to enjoy school. I attended Our Lady of Guadalupe Catholic School in Bakersfield. My brother had moved on to middle school at Garces Memorial, Bakersfield's only Catholic secondary school. It was through him that I got a preview of what lay ahead for me. He spoke to me about his new experiences in class as well as extracurricular activities, such as track and music in which he excelled. Some of his stories were so funny we fell asleep laughing in the room we shared.

After years of putting to good use our home Britannica and World Book encyclopedias, as well as the illustrated King James Bible, I began going regularly to the small City library on Baker Street, rain or shine. It was built in 1915 and funded by Andrew Carnegie, a successful rags-to-riches industrialist who funded public libraries in hundreds of American cities in the early 1900s. The library's fine collection of over 10,000 books was augmented by the main library downtown, and the librarians were friendly and helpful to me in finding sources for my growing span of eclectic interests. Before long, I was adept at using the Dewey Decimal System, and had learned to use the digests which helped me to chart my future course.

The cozy library was a microcosm of the huge world that awaited me. It held me in awe.

Our family belonged to Our Lady of Guadalupe Church, a Catholic parish in Bakersfield. Having adopted the library as my sanctuary, I slowly began losing interest in attending Catholic Mass, church Holy Days, and all the other trappings of the church, although I still served as an altar boy. In our weekly religious talks, Father Küster had become more and more authoritarian and demeaning at every turn of the new changes being made in the Church by Pope John XXIII and Vatican Council II. Being a stalwart in the traditional ways, I think he felt the Church was losing its grip on its hierarchy as well as the once faithful "flock." I knew the latter to be true.

Despite one's theological perspective, the folksinger, Bob Dylan, aptly put it when he sang that the answers "were blowin' in the wind." And at Our Lady of Guadalupe, the nuns, especially the younger ones, were excited about the changes, and their joy was contagious.

But, in spite of my increasing questioning of the Church, there were yet to be a few more altar boy adventures before Father Burkhart relieved me of my duties for going AWOL in the seventh grade.

In order to not give the wrong impression, i.e. that most of my experiences as an altar boy were bizarre, strange, or anything other than moments of dedication and true devotion—innocent as they may have been—let me just say that while I was at Our Lady of Guadalupe, for most years, I was a devout Catholic. Before the seventh grade, I wanted to become a Divine Word missionary priest and go to Africa to serve in a mission. Sometimes I think that the desire may have had more to do with the fantasy of wearing an ankle-length, brilliant white cassock, and a crucifix hanging from my neck.

To be fair to myself, however, the more noble intention of my ambition was to help those in need by any means necessary, while drawing them away from "paganism" and "voodoo-type superstitions." The ultimate goal was to convert them to Catholicism. As I look back on it, I realize there was absolutely no original thinking involved, that it was simply a reflection of what I had been exposed to and led to believe. But it was a path, one I considered while at Guadalupe.

I used to serve as an altar boy at Mass with a boy named Benny. But weeks had passed since I had served Mass with Benny. He had chosen to serve at weddings and encouraged me to do likewise. There was "good money in it" because of the "tips" one got, he told me. The tips I guess, were part of the Mexican tradition, much like that of "*bolo*," after baptisms. *Bolo* is that Mexican tradition where after the baptism, the *padrino* (godfather) throws a generous amount of coins in the air so that all the children in attendance can catch or scramble for them. I, however, preferred to serve at funerals because it took me out of a class that I often found to be unbearably boring. Also, weddings were often on Saturdays, and my Saturdays had become my library days when I spent hours at the library on Baker Street, poring over books, maps, magazines, and anything else I discovered. For others, like Benny, Saturdays were for weddings.

Then, there came a funeral for which my regular partner was absent, and it was Benny who covered for him. It was, therefore, by chance that Benny and I served together again, and it was to be our last time.

It was a relatively small funeral and Father Riordan, our fiery Irish priest, rushed through the service in his booming voice as no other priest could. He then left hurriedly to visit an ill parishioner who was hospitalized to administer her the Last Rites.

As he rushed out, he instructed Benny and me to clear the altar of items used in the Mass, as the *ancianas*, or elderly women volunteers, would be stripping the altar of its linens.

We did as he asked, then I went to change out of my cassock and surplice in the room opposite from the Sacristy, where the priests dressed and kept their vestments and Mass implements.

Benny stayed behind.

Then, as I was changing, he ran in yelling, "Eloy! Eloy! Eloy come here, quickly!"

"Why?" I asked guardedly.

"Bones from Rome!" he fired back as he rushed out.

Stepping into the altar area, I saw Benny's torso resting on the altar with his legs dangling wildly. I saw that the altar linens had already been removed, leaving the altar top completely bare.

Benny was directly over the area that priests kiss at the time of consecrating the bread and wine—converting it to the Body and Blood of Christ.

"Benny, what are you doing?" I asked.

He was clawing desperately at a cutout fitted smack in the middle of the stone altar top. It was a square-shaped board, measuring approximately a square foot. He had no fingernails to speak of, so his fingers were raw from his attempts at removing it. Benny was the nervous type who constantly chewed on his nails.

"Quick, help me!" Benny whispered.

My curiosity got the best of me. I looked toward the Sacristy door before whispering to him, "Move over! Do you have a pocket-knife?"

He immediately whipped one out and handed it to me. I chose the strongest blade.

"Okay, now give me a boost."

Using his clasped hands as a stirrup, I raised myself to the altar and carefully inserted the blade into the narrow space at the lowest corner. It worked. I was able to then lift the board and lay it aside.

I looked into the altar top. "Benny, look at this! How did you know?"

Inside the hollow space about ten inches in depth, there were numerous glass vials, arranged in no particular manner. Each contained what appeared to be pieces of bone, dried-up skin, cloth, and hair. Some of the vials were labeled with the names of saints, finely handwritten on old parchment. None of those names stand out now.

"Move over!" Benny demanded.

I lowered myself to the floor, and he climbed back up. Once more I checked all the church doors. I could only hear the hushed voices of the *ancianas* just outside.

We were safe, but for how long?

When I turned to Benny, he had slowly started removing the vials; one by one.

"Just want a closer look..."

"Benny, are you crazy?" were my parting words to him.

I'd seen enough.

I quickly exited the church out the back door and waded into a sea of screaming kids just out of Guadalupe school for recess.

For a while afterward, I was lost in reflection. The remains had a disturbing impact on me, triggering what seemed like *déjà vu*.

For centuries, the Roman Catholic Church had a monopoly on the sales of relics. The sin of "simony" encompasses the unauthorized sale of saints' remains; everything from body organs, teeth, clothing, and flesh.

Having been initiated into the Roman Catholic Church in the Pre-Vatican Council II days, I'm aware that what was taught in Catholic schools in this regard was cursory and superficial. The veneration of relics displayed or hidden under an altar top, such as we had brought to light, was justified or simply grouped with things "best left to one's devotion and faith."

Also, having previously witnessed the mummified, impregnated nuns, who had been plastered alive within the walls of Mexico City's Colonia San Ángel, the hidden relics only added to my suspicions of the Catholic Church, which I now viewed as macabre and more akin to witchcraft.

Despite my prayers, doubt continued to fester in me, and I decided it would be best to leave the Church.

Thus, began my spiritual diaspora.

4.

Despite Mom's heavy workload she always found time to do fun things outside the home with us. We would go to local restaurants such as Bill Lee's, Arizona Cafe, and Norriega's. We would go to the movies and attend cultural events and concerts, as well as make trips to Hart Park and Morro Bay to get away from the scorching summer heat. These were all fun, except perhaps, going to my brother's piano recitals. But of all of these, my favorite trip was going to the Kern County Fair, which took place in the early fall. The 1959 visit to the fair is the one that stands out the most. It was the fall I started the fourth grade. It began rather normally, but then it took a strange twist.

When we arrived and saw all the cows, chickens, and sheep, we were brought back to memories of *abuelita's* farm in Chihuahua. Here the farm animals were all groomed by their young 4-H sponsors, girls and boys in brilliant white uniforms. One of them reminded me of a pretty, blond Mormon girl from Chuíchupa, where *tía* Carmen and *tío* Ezequiel lived.

With cotton candy, corn dogs, and sodas in hand, we then went through the other exhibits focusing on the plants and landscaping for Mom, and the rocks and minerals for my brother and me.

As for the rides, Mom only went on the Ferris Wheel and bumper cars. Florencio and I rode the fast rides like "The Hammer" and the "Tilt-a-Whirl." We laughed hysterically as we stumbled about, dizzy and giddy from being spun around. Mom waited for us, worried, hugging us as we exited the gate. My brother, three years older, resisted any of Mom's public displays of affection, or *cariños*. But I didn't yet. When I did later, I came to justify it by thinking it was a normal part of growing up.

During my childhood, Mom tried to fill the roles of both mother and father, but with time, I set out seeking a surrogate father. It was to be a long and painful process, after which I settled on the words "call no man upon earth your father, for your father is in heaven"— the first meaning any man, including biological father; the second meaning one's heavenly father.

The games—where one could win anything from a plate or a goldfish, to a canary or a huge stuffed animal—were mostly of Florencio's liking, and he was good at them. Mom and I would cheer him on, embarrassing him.

My favorite attraction was the "freak show." It was there, where the year before, we had seen a sword swallower, a tiny Siamese twin in a jar of formaldehyde, a man totally tattooed and pierced, the captivating "Lady from Shanghai," and a 500-pound mountain of a woman.

Mom didn't particularly like for me to be exposed to these exhibitions. She uttered, "We're all children of God." She did, however, make me promise on the way, "But son, after that we'll go, okay?

"Si mamá."

At the end of the game alley were the "House of Horrors," "House of Mirrors," and the freak show. It was late by then and many people were driving out of the nearby parking lot. The dead-end was suffocating; the smells of gasoline fumes, animal dung, hay, and dirt, all combining with the Bakersfield hot air.

As we approached, I noticed that along with the normal gawkers, there were others that appeared to be just loitering without any apparent purpose. They did not seem unfriendly, just different. I believe they felt safer in this corner of the fair, their own dead-end corner.

It was exciting. The carnival barkers, each tightly holding a microphone close to his mouth, loudly incited us to dare go past the curtains and into the "freak show."

"Step right in kids—ladies, and gentlemen!"

"Walk right up and get your tickets from this lovely LADY!"

"Don't be squeamish!"

The high-pitched cacophony blended with the laughter and growl of loud generators behind the exhibits, and glaring lights reflected off the large, colorful painted images of the featured "freaks." I stood there completely captivated and anxious to go in.

Mom's attention was immediately drawn to one feature in particular.

"THE LAST OF THE AZTECS!"

Above the words was a painting of what looked to be a wizard. Seated on a pedestal was the presumed Aztec, on his head a large wizard's cone hat with shiny stars, comets, and the moon and sun. Draping him was a brilliant maroon cloak, and he was resting a magic wand on his lap.

We entered the exhibition tent. Greeting us just past the curtain was a glass-encased bust of a gypsy, dressed as brightly as Mom did when she was a fortune teller at the Mexican Independence Day celebrations. She did it to raise money for the non-profit she was secretary of, the *Comisión Honorífica Mexicana,* an organization for Mexican immigrants. This fortune teller though was eerie, made of porcelain but with very convincing facial features. Its bright eyes followed one's movement.

Mom led us to where there was a contortionist. He was a scantily dressed Indian fakir who could bend his arms, legs, and body in the most amazing positions. His dark, penetrating eyes pierced into mine.

I whispered to Florencio how much quieter it was inside the tent compared to outside, but he did not respond.

We walked past the fakir's partition wall and there, sitting on a pedestal, was the featured "Aztec."

The Last of the Aztecs was much smaller than he appeared in the painting outside. His cloak was worn and stained by what appeared to be old food stains. His head was very small in comparison to the rest of his body, a "pin-head" is what I overheard. He was half-asleep and his round face expressionless. Although he drooled, he held onto his magic wand with his small, puffy hand.

While I stared, Mom told us to stay there, and that she would be right back, leaving Florencio and I standing there. The "Aztec" did not stir. In fact, he was snoring.

Mom returned with an older man and began asking him questions.

"Who is this man you call the last of the Aztecs? Is he ill? Where is his family? And why is he asleep!" Mom insisted.

The man lost his composure, and his face turned red with anger.

"Look, ma'am, what gives you the right to ask me these questions, anyway? Who are youthe police?"

"No. But that's exactly where I'm going tomorrow morning—to the police, to the county health department, to the district attorney's office, and..."

Mom appeared to be getting angry, standing toe-to-toe with a man three times her size. The man's huge red wide-eyed face no longer looked angry, just stunned.

"Look, lady, let's be reasonable here. I'll refund your money."

Mom grabbed my hand and motioned to my brother.

"You've not seen the last of me. And, you better let this man rest."

It was a quiet ride home. Mom hardly said a word. Florencio and I talked excitedly about the rides, but conversation stopped when the Aztec man came up.

The next day was a school day so Florencio and I got up early and went through our usual routine before darting off to school. Later in the day when I arrived home, I saw that Mom's car was still in the driveway, and momentarily I feared she might be ill. She had her own business, but very rarely would she be home at four o'clock in the afternoon unless she was sick, feeling very melancholy, or *tío* Yb was visiting from Los Angeles. Except for her bouts with depression, these were rare occasions.

When I ran in, she was sitting at the kitchen table and on the phone. She gave me a big smile as she pointed to the mouthpiece. Not quite understanding, I smiled back and went to my room to take off my school uniform and get into my jeans.

She later told me that the man at the fair was going to be investigated by the Mexican General Consul (*Cónsul General*) in Fresno, located a couple of hours north of Bakersfield, as well as by the local District Attorney's office.

"That's good news, right?"

"Yes, son. At first, they gave me the runaround, but when I asked to personally see the *Cónsul General*, they put him on the phone. They're going to send somebody down here."

I had not seen her so happy in a long time.

"I'm still waiting to hear back from the health department."

Mom was not a novice when it came to defending herself, or others. As a seamstress for US Army officers in Fort Bliss and White Sands, she worked under a tyrannical and racist forewoman, a Ms. Tidwell, from Oklahoma. The department was made up of twelve Mexican-American women, some who had been subjected to her abusive behavior long before Mom.

Mom had packed parachutes in Arizona during the Korean War and was proud to have received several awards and commendations. She'd had a great foreman then. But under Ms. Tidwell she witnessed and was subjected to the very worst, including the throwing of scissors! When angry, Ms. Tidwell would often use profanity and racial epithets.

But for my mother, the last straw was when a sergeant at the base admitted to her that Ms. Tidwell had sold Mom's phone number to him for a large can of coffee. He admitted that to Mom out of fear and remorse after he made the mistake of calling her for a date.

The next day Mom marched in alone to see the Fort Bliss brigadier general. In her broken English, as she put it, he listened while she ran down the long list of grievances of all her co-workers and herself, including the most recent incident involving the sergeant. The next day, to the surprise of Mom's elated co-workers, their forewoman, who had more than twenty years seniority, was discharged from the Army.

Later in the week, after many phone calls, plus visits back to the fairgrounds to meet with a county official and a consular investigator, Mom gave Florencio and I a summary of events relating to the man we knew only as the "Last of the Aztecs."

It turned out the man with the red face was in deep trouble. It was found that he had bought the "Aztec" man in Mexico. The man had been born with microcephaly, a condition in which a baby's head is significantly smaller than normal, and as a result he had serious mental disabilities. Because he was a Mexican citizen, the Mexican Consulate in Fresno immediately applied to the court for custody and they were making arrangements to have him placed in an orphanage in his home state of Michoacán. As for the health department, it found numerous violations of health and safety regulations for which the owner was cited and eventually fined.

Weeks later the consulate informed Mom that the freak show had been shut down.

In the following years, Mom got involved with other social issues.

After she was denied the purchase of a house in a new housing development in South Bakersfield, the realtor, John Shipman, admitted to us that the reason for the denial was that we were Mexican. A couple of years later, at the prompting of Doctor Fuller, our family physician, Mom became very active in California's Rumford Fair Housing Act campaign. California eventually made it illegal to discriminate on the basis of race and national origin in the sale and rental of real estate.

Though my brother and I would revisit the Kern County Fair, we never again went down the game alley to see the shows. I also never again used the terms "freak" or "freak show" until now, in recounting the story of the "Last of the Aztecs."

5.

For years I saw the girls at Guadalupe school in their blue skirts, white blouses, and on cold winter days, red sweaters with a school emblem patch. We, in turn, wore navy blue cords, blue shirts, and matching red sweaters. Day in and day out, for nine months out of the year, we went to the same classes, ate lunch in the same cafeteria, used the same confessionals, knelt and worshipped at the same altar. Day in and day out, we were as close as family.

Then, within a matter of months, childhood was forever gone, and adolescence arrived with seventh grade. I did not fully realize what I was undergoing, but I was mindful of the beauty evolving around me. For me, the focus of attention was Leanor Martinez. She captivated me with her broad, friendly smile, bright blue eyes, chestnut brown hair, and bubbling self-confidence. She was also very bright. There were other girls I took an interest in while at Guadalupe, but none made the same impression on me that she did.

During seventh and eighth grades at Guadalupe, the hushed gossip between the girls and their emergency trips out to the restroom slowly evolved to the more mature notes that began to circulate. Predating the social media of today, these notes were just as captivating. They announced new couples, told of jealousies, break-ups, set territorial parameters, or simply flirted, with hearts and arrows that jumped out at you.

The nuns might have been pleased with the penmanship, if not the notes themselves, which the nuns confiscated quickly, reprimanding the culprits immediately, or keeping them after class. Sometimes, the note would be read out loud, and what followed was a flushed face and teary eyes for the offender.

The seventh grade for me brought on many changes. I was twelve years old. At the start of the 1962-1963 school year, Father Burkhart came to my class one fall day and in a very friendly, unceremonious manner, dismissed me from the altar boys. I had failed to serve another morning Mass and so I was expecting it. I had just outgrown it. I had found other ways to escape a boring class other than serving funeral Masses and taking field trips to the cemetery.

In my five years as an altar boy I was able to learn much. I saw much suffering and grief at the funeral Masses and burials I attended. I stored abundant memories of the myriad of expressions of grief, the weeping, wailing, as well as expressions of love and affection. I recall too, the restrained expressions of those who keep, or attempt to keep, their suffering locked inside of them without apparent faith, or consolation.

By serving funeral Masses I was required to be absent from school for about two hours, but being with Father Burkhart was both educational and fun in itself. He never dwelled in doctrinal teachings as did Father Küster. In the years I assisted him with funerals he spoke to me of many interesting things, including Greek Mythology—its colorful gods and goddesses and their adventures. He also told me of his love for the Church and his experiences in the seminary. He was perhaps the main reason why in the fifth and sixth grades I considered becoming a priest.

My altar boy days simply fell away much like the leaves outside my classroom window. I only regretted not having been more open with Father Burkhart.

The seventh-grade classroom was right behind the grotto of Our Lady of Guadalupe, not far from the rectory, and my desk situated in the back of the class was right next to the window. It was perfect. It was through that window that I developed the skill of daydreaming. One of my favorite methods was by focusing on the rhythmic sound of the sprinkler just outside. It assisted me in entering a hypnotic trance whenever I so chose.

One day Mom announced to my brother and me that she had made an appointment for us to go see Father Riordon the following Saturday.

"See him about what?" I was the first to ask, suspecting I might be in some sort of trouble. Florencio liked to play Mom's enforcer where I was concerned. So, I was often careful when discussing some things with him. Florencio took his role way too seriously, but I loved him anyway.

"Well, you both are coming of age now and I think it would be good for you to have a frank and open discussion with a man; to ask him any questions you may have."

"Discussion about what?" I pressed her.

My brother Florencio did not seem at all interested. In fact, the year before Mom had given him a book for his fifteenth birthday, On Becoming a Man, which I knew he had not read. I read it twice. It was Christian in its orientation and glossed over some things. I would have preferred a "how-to" on winning the love of a girl, but no luck.

"Things I don't feel capable of discussing with you."

This did not come as a big surprise to me as I had overheard a recent phone conversation she had with our uncle, Yb. She confided to him that during years of playing the dual role of mother and father she was certain she would be able to guide us in all matters having to do with our coming of age. But now, she confessed, she'd found she couldn't do it. I wished she would relegate that role to our Uncle Yb, but fat chance, he was a committed bachelor, a "playboy" right out of the Heffner playbook.

Years earlier, I had given up on ever having a father, even a substitute. I recall even now how embarrassing it was to blurt out "father!" to a family friend when we were on a family river outing. I was about ten years old then and I would rather the Kern River had swallowed me up.

For this task Mom had chosen the most virile of our three priests—the fiery Irishman, Father Riordon.

Our meeting in the rectory with Father Riordon went faster than a typical medical examination, quick and perfunctory. He spoke metaphorically of "seeds" and such. Much like Florencio's book on the topic, he was no help.

"How could he be?" I asked myself. "Did he not take a vow of chastity from a young age?"

When Mom picked us up, she asked how it had gone. She seemed happy that we went through with it. Florencio merely shrugged his shoulders and went right back to practicing his piano lessons. My response? Well, let's just say it was quick and perfunctory.

The days dragged on and I got nowhere with Leanor. I was shy, insecure, and awkward. I suspect that Leanor caught me looking at her at times, probably misinterpreting my attitude for disinterest, aloofness, or worst yet, vanity. Nothing could have been further from the truth. But then, apparently, I was mute too.

Mom was as insightful as she was perceptive. One afternoon, she asked how things were going at school. It was then I revealed to her my feelings about Leanor. Sensing my angst, she pondered what I said, smiled, and told me rather seriously—

"*Hijo*, I have taught you to respect girls, not fear them."

Soon afterward, the inevitable happened. Leanor found a boyfriend. He was also in our class, a friend actually—as much as all of us boys were friends—and in a strange kind of way, it made it easier.

At any rate, the pressure was off as I realized that I was not yet competitive in these matters of the heart.

At the end of the seventh grade, after being denied the purchase of the home, Mom and I drove around looking for a house to buy closer to school. After hours of looking one Saturday, I spotted a for-sale sign partially hidden by rich green shrubbery. It was a white, Spanish-style home built in 1936, matching the architecture of the Bakersfield Inn that sat across the street. The roof was Spanish tile and the yard had large Callery Pear, black walnut, maple and evergreen trees.

Within days Mom's offer was accepted by the owners, who also happened to be the owners of the Bakersfield Inn, which was soon to be sold as well. The owners, a Jewish gay couple, had suddenly decided to relocate to Los Angeles and had left their *mezuzah* nailed to the front door post. I did not have any idea what a *mezuzah* was, but my natural curiosity took hold when home alone one day after we had moved in. I carefully opened the small metal case decorated with a Hebrew Shin and Star of David. I pried loose the small rolled parchment contained in it and placed it on the dining room table. I did not know Hebrew, but I did recognize the hand-drawn lettering as such. The next day I brought it to my merchant friend, Mr. Hirschfield, who was Jewish.

The small haberdashery on Baker Street was a classic example of ordered chaos, with items stacked high to its rafters. In the midst of all of this sat Mr. Hirschfield.

I had first met him in 1962. He and his wife, both in their sixties, owned the small clothing store on the same block as Mother's bakery. These two businesses were on my short-list of stopovers on my frequent trips to the library, just a few blocks away. In one I got my donuts and in the other, invaluable conversation. From time to time I also bought a shirt or other items from Mr. Hirschfield, but that came from me and he never encouraged it. I enjoyed his company.

"Hello, Eloy. How are you today, young man?"

I reached deep in my pocket and brought out the *mezuzah* to show him. I was both nervous and excited, trusting that Mr. Hirschfield would soon reveal the mystery.

"What is that?" he asked and before I answered, he reached out, looked at me, and said, "May I see it?"

"Yes," I said excitedly.

He took it in his hands, and examined it, "Eloy, this is a *mezuzah*. Where did you get it?"

"From our new house on Pershing Street," I answered.

"Oh yes, you told me you were moving closer," he responded.

"What is a *mezuzah*?" I asked.

"Where was it?" Mr. Hirschfield asked.

"It was nailed onto our front door," I said.

"Did you read it?" he asked, smiling.

"No. I can't. That's why I brought it to you. Can you please read it for me?"

Mr. Hirschfield put on his serious expression and walked over to his small cluttered desk in the back of his cramped store. He sat down and put on his "binocular" reading glasses, carefully opened the *mezuzah* from which he took the parchment out, and then gently opened it with both hands. He read to me and then translated, in Hebrew and then English, in his heavy German accent.

Before I left, I learned of many things, for example; Passover, fidelity to God, protection of one's household. He told me about how, in the Book of Deuteronomy, the Jewish people were instructed to proclaim their faith to the one true God by placing quoted scripture in a *mezuzah* nailed to their doorposts. From time to time, Mr. Hirschfield held it between his thumb and index finger, emphasizing what he was telling me.

"Eloy, I do not know why this was left behind. But it is a blessing to you and your family. Guard it well."

"I will, Mr. Hirschfield. I'll put it back where it was."

"Good."

He handed it back to me and I walked out in a daze from all I had learned. The time had passed so quickly that it was near dark, and so I headed home.

I did not stop to see Mr. Hirschfield after that for some time, but we would often wave to each other as I passed his store. The memory of him smiling at me through his shop window is a powerful image from my childhood.

6.

Because of Mom's hard work and natural competitive nature, her bakery, *La Bonita,* prospered, and overtook much of its competition. The man who owned *Casa Tortillas*, the only other mechanized tortilla factory, and who had been around years before *La Bonita*, grew weary of the rat race and closed up shop. We quickly settled into a comfortable, middle-class lifestyle in our new home.

My brother had already begun to immerse himself in classical music. He was taught by the best teachers; Mr. Tarnovsky in Los Angeles and Mrs. Shaver in Bakersfield. I had long ago given up the thought of following in his footsteps. I did not have it in me to practice the long hours he did. During the week he would practice up to four hours a day, and on the weekends, double that.

I had detested performing in recitals. When in El Paso, we were both students of Mrs. Michaels, who was not only nice to us but on several Sundays invited us to attend her Protestant church service. Mom believed the more experiences we had in this regard, the better. So, before we left for Bakersfield, we had to perform in her annual student piano recital at the El Paso main library. Mom bought us matching silk suits for our first recital. They were grey but looked silver with their silken sheen.

For days my nerves had been building up. As for my brother, he was as cool as a bullfighter, or managed to conceal any anxiety. My piece was to be "The Caissons Go Rolling Along," a military march. My brother, on the other hand, was to play a more advanced civilian selection. It was to be a night recital, which only added to my angst.

As is normally the case in these torturous student exhibitions, the beginners are selected to open the show. I was selected. I waited in the first row of the small auditorium for my introduction, music in hand, perspiring, and fidgeting.

Then I was called by Mrs. Michaels to sit at the Steinway concert grand piano at the center of the stage.

Being as I just wanted to get it over with, I rushed up the stairs. Not slowing down at all, I leaped up and landed hard on the polished bench. As I slid, I found nothing to grab so I kept sliding the full length of it. Somehow, I was able to land on my feet in a semi-crouched position. My new shoes made a sharp bang upon landing. I still clutched my page of sheet music.

The audience immediately roared with laughter for what seemed like minutes. There followed encouraging applause, I assumed.

After a rather frantic rendition of "Caissons" that evening, I decided not to put myself through this, ever again. Florencio, however, gave it his all and for his hard work and dedication, he got a Chickering Baby Grand just like his idol, French-Canadian pianist Glenn Gould.

Our eighth-grade classroom was newly built and conveniently located adjacent to the school cafeteria, across the street from the church, convent, and the classrooms for grades one through seven. Just being there was a constant reminder that in nine months or less, I would be moving on. My friends would be going to any of several Bakersfield public high schools. For me though, it would be another four years of Catholic education at Garces Memorial High School, unless I could prevail in the matter. My argument was honest and truthful, basically that at Bakersfield High School, one of the public high schools, they had a vastly larger selection of pre-college courses. I knew this because I had studied the school's catalog.

When Mom rejected this idea, "What about the seminary then?" was my next volley.

"Hijo que vas hacer en un seminario lejos de aquí? Espérate mejor cuatro años como te dijo el padre." (Son, what will you do in a seminary far from here? Better to wait four years like the father said.)

"Que padre? Si Ustéd me ha dicho que nuestro padre está en el cielo?" I teased her. (What father? You've told me that our Father is in heaven?)

"Eloy, no te hagas el muy vivo he? Ya te he dicho que no—y no." (Eloy, don't act so smart, okay? I've told you "no" and that's that.)

I knew she'd spoken the last word on the subject.

So much for that. Just recently a priest recruiter from the Divine Word Missionaries Seminary in Riverside, California, had come to speak to us in response to the inquiry I had sent. Although his opinion was that it might be best if I waited until after I graduated from Garces High, I suspected that Mom had prepped him before his arrival. Our Colonna blood may have well been Machiavellian too, judging by how Mom operated behind the scenes at times. My fate had been sealed.

In the second week of eighth-grade, we went to the "*Fiestas Patrias*," the Mexican Independence Day celebration held at the Kern County Fairgrounds.

The musical program was put on by Maria Elena Anderson and her daughter, Cathy. Maria Elena was a popular KWAC radio personality, and her program was both well organized and professional. The Los Angeles band Lalo Guerrero was featured and they were great. Maria Elena and her younger sister, Rebecca, were friends of my mother's and were together laughing, "*tijereando*," and awhile dancing with Father Ford. Years later Mom and Maria Elena would have a falling-out over my mother's strong and open support of the UFW and opposition to the Teamsters Union. Several years later my mother would fund her own program at KWAC, *La Voz del Pueblo* (The People's Voice.)

Leanor was there, too, with her younger sister, Henrietta, and her parents. The highlight of the evening was when she and her sister passed by me and Leanor smiled and said hello. This simple, friendly gesture lifted me and I realized how it had been three months since I had seen her, and how I had missed her.

My mother had heard from mutual acquaintances how involved Leonor's parents were in a community organization called the Community Services Organization (CSO). Both were founding members and her father, Henry Martinez, was the president. I never imagined that seventeen years later, when working with the United Farm Workers (UFW) and attending a CSO anniversary dinner in Bakersfield, Cesar would tell me he knew them from his early days of organizing and counted them as good friends and supporters.

Father Ford, our new priest, continued having a great time all evening, drinking beer and dancing with his parishioners. Father Riordon was there too, but mostly drinking, smoking, and talking with the men.

As for me, however, the call to the priesthood would have to wait.

7.

Sister Mary Dolores was a great teacher. She would get angry at times, but it never seemed to dampen her genuine joy in teaching us; no small task with a class of forty. Personally, Sister Dolores accommodated me in one particular way, for which I was grateful to her. She made a note about tardiness on my first report card, which became an issue at home. From the first day of school, Mom had impressed upon me that my conduct grade was the most important. Having seen the tardiness comment on my report card, she was starting to notice how they might have been correlated.

"Que haces con tu tiempo, muchacho?" (What do you do with your time, young man?)

The fact of the matter was that I had discovered late-night television, such as Johnny Carson, and Joe Pyke, as well as news and panel shows.

"Estás viendo demasiada televisión. Pero ya no! Se acabaron esos días." (You're watching too much television. But that's it! Those days are gone!) Mom could be so dramatic.

Translation to Sister Dolores: "Sister, I have an eye and sleeping condition that Mom's looking into."

The accommodation: I was moved to the back of the room so that when late, which was almost daily, I did not disturb the other students.

Sister Mary Dolores played another role in my life that year, when on a cold November morning during recess she broke the news that President Kennedy had been assassinated. She sent us home early to pray and grieve. Over the next four days, the television would be our teacher. Like millions of others, I remained mesmerized by the public news coverage of a very public assassination. Then, Florencio and I saw live the execution of Oswald by Jack Ruby; without knowing about the "dots," or even less so, about how they might be connected.

A few days later, upon our return to school, Miss Edna Tilyer, our school music teacher, told my Mom and us boys that as she was going home from school that morning, walking past the front of our church, a man dressed in a dark business suit and tie rushed by on his way up the church stairs, muttering to himself, "We killed him…We killed him." She said she had never seen this mysterious man before that day, and never saw him again.

Those were strange days indeed, and it was the music of the Beatles that would greet us on the other side of grief and help us to heal. Sister Dolores even joined in the craze when the Beatles took some in our class by storm. Her love of their music is part of what led me to embrace them. Their songs matched my every mood. The lyrics tutored me in those matters of the heart I found mysterious and for me, at least, there was an immediate connection.

"Have you ever cupped a firefly in your hands and seen its glow?"

The rest of the eighth grade was relatively uneventful except for the fire at the Bakersfield Inn and resultant closure of the bridge I took to school each day, and our graduation dance.

During the last two years at Our Lady of Guadalupe school, I would always cross the iconic Bakersfield Inn bridge. It spanned the width of Union Avenue, old Highway 99. One afternoon, coming from school, I walked over the bridge when I saw a plume of black smoke coming from the restaurant kitchen window of the Inn. Not thinking much of it, I continued on, walked down the stairs into the Inn's lobby and out past a wing of rooms. After I settled in at home, I heard numerous fire engines out on my street. When I went out to see, the fire was raging.

Sad times those were, too. However, I was relieved that our house and the *mezuzah* were spared. As Mr. Hirschfield told me, "In a way, it marked your own Passover." As things were looking, it might also have marked my passing into adolescence. The last day I would ever visit the haberdashery was when I went to buy graduation shoes. Mom got me the suit, tie, and shirt, but I insisted on getting the shoes myself with my allowance, and from Mr. Hirschfield.

I had procrastinated and went to get them the day before the ceremony. This was to be the last shopping necessary. I walked in so fast that the little bell hanging from the store door rang more like a *Sanctus* bell. Mr. Hirschfield had not been well for months and it took him some time to come out from the back.

"Mr. Hirschfield, I need to buy shoes for my graduation," I said.

"Hello, Eloy. Have a seat there, please," he responded. "What kind of shoes are you looking for?"

"Beatle boots," I eagerly replied.

I immediately began describing them, as well as telling him about the Beatles. He at first looked at me as if I were from Mars, but quickly caught on to my description. He asked me to help him move some boxes out of the way, and then picked one off the shelf.

"Is this what you're looking for? They're Spanish boots."

They were perfect, so I bought them.

Mr. Hirschfield put them in a bag and walked me toward the door.

"Congratulations, Eloy. I may not be here too much longer, but I wish you all the best."

As I was walking out, I looked back and thanked him. He smiled back. It wasn't until I walked away from his store that I got a chill; one like the one that I got on Christmas Eve, when *abuelita* Domitila passed away at Mom's home in Bakersfield.

The next day would be my final compulsory church attendance. In our red caps and gowns, sitting shoulder-to-shoulder, my friends and I looked like rookie cardinals in St. Peter's basilica.

Many memories, both good and bad, came to mind, namely; my arrival from Texas in the third grade, the early altar boy days, all the kind nuns and priests, "The Last of the Aztecs," May's morning prayers and singing at the grotto for our Lady, our move to Pershing Street, and yes, even the Roman relics and dreaded confessions.

I reminisced, knowing that it was time to move on and leave Our Lady of Guadalupe school behind. But, as I was to find out, there was one last remaining matter before it all could come to full closure.

Before I knew it, we had all moved to the cafeteria, diplomas in hand. Today, the cafeteria would serve a different purpose. It was colorfully decorated for the graduation dance, with streamers, balloons, and bright tablecloths.

I had never danced before, so I was nervous.

I mingled with my friends and surveyed the hall. The girls did the same. All my friends were quick in picking partners and getting out on the dance floor. I, however, continued standing and watching—frozen. Benny, who had four older sisters, had been well taught; he spun like a top and with much ease. I concluded that the best dancers were those who had either hosted parties or had been to them. But those with older sisters seemed to be the best. I had neither sisters nor had I been to any dance parties, which is why I remained standing there. I may as well have been nailed to the floor.

Events all passed in an instant when I saw Leanor smiling at me. I made up my mind that come hell or high water, I would dance with her. I decided it would have to be a slow dance. I wanted to get close to her, hoping any blunders on my part would be less conspicuous. I would be quite wrong about that.

As the evening wore on and each song played, I began to fear I'd miss my opportunity.

Then came "Tell Him" (a song by Patti Drew). I made my way to Leanor. She hadn't missed a dance it seemed, so I caught her resting.

"Leanor, will you dance with me?"

"Yes."

During our dance, I lost sense of time. Even under the watchful eyes of our beautifully dressed mothers, the world shut off for me; even in spite of Benny's rude, loud whisper,

"Eloy, you have to move around!" As he motioned with his right hand and index finger, in a wide circular pattern, I remained unshaken and centered.

The truth is, I felt as if I was on fire, and it had all started with our hands. Even through her sheer gloves, I could feel our hands were wet with perspiration, I felt the wild galloping of our hearts getting stronger. We didn't say a thing until it was over. I was speechless.

When the dance was over, I walked Leanor to where her mother sat, and thanked her. She gave me one of her shy, friendly smiles. It was a smile I haven't seen since, for I never saw her again.

For me, the long day had ended; so too, our years together at Guadalupe.

Through the years I have remembered Leanor quite fondly. It was she, after all, who helped me cross the threshold into adulthood.

"The art of cupping a firefly in your hands is in its safe release."

8.

When I filled out my application to Garces Memorial High School (Garces), my full name was required.

"Mom, I don't have a middle name, do I?"

"Yes, you do, it's Eloy."

"Eloy? Well, what's my first name then?"

"Your *abuelita* Domitíla gave you the name 'Eloy' at birth, and I gave you the name 'Marco' later. Your grandmother got your name from the Old Testament, and I gave you the name 'Marco' because it was the name of an Argentine singer I loved. So, your name is Marco Eloy."

"What?" I told myself, cradling my head in my hands and looking down at the form.

While filling out that simple form and asking more questions, I uncovered more family mysteries. Apparently, my mother did not attend my baptism, only my Dad and my godfather, Don Manuel "Manuelito" Elías.

I knew Manuelito to be an eccentric, wealthy bachelor and a rancher from Sonora, Mexico. He was my Dad's cousin and related to former Mexican president, Plutarco Elías Calles. During his presidency in the 1930s, President Elías Calles had enforced certain federal laws limiting the number of clerics and other religious staff, as well as closing down Catholic schools. In protest, the Church closed down all its churches. This resulted in the "*Cristero* Revolt," a three-year war resulting in over seventy-thousand deaths.

My baptism was conducted in a Catholic church in Douglas, Arizona, and my Dad came back home with a baptismal certificate to prove it.

The other thing Mom told me about my baptism was that I did not have a godmother, a *madrina*. And *madrinas* are sacrosanct in the Mexican culture.

Okay, I thought, a godless *padrino* connection is one thing, but no *madrina*?

I was off to a shaky start, I thought. I'd better not ask any further questions lest I be denied admission to Bakersfield's citadel of Catholic education.

Everything turned out fine, however, and I was admitted to Garces as a freshman in the fall of 1964.

The school sat atop a beautifully landscaped hill in what was then the most affluent residential area of the city, not far from Panorama Drive. It was quite a contrast to the barrios of East Bakersfield, "La Loma" and "El Okie," which in turn compared to the poorest black neighborhood surrounding Cottonwood Road.

Aside from the regular tuition paid by parents, I suspect the school was funded predominantly by the local growers: Banducci, Bidart, Giumarra, and others, whose children attended the school.

My estimate is that the makeup of Garces, in the four years I attended, was about 75% white, 20% Mexican-American and about 5% black. The students, well-taught and disciplined by the school's dedicated instructors, were mostly Catholic and loyal fans of the school football team, the Rams.

Among the school's mandatory classes was religion: Religion I,

II, III, and IV, freshman through senior years. While the emphasis of these classes concerned the teaching of church dogma and the study of scripture, the better part of it for me was the practical application of scriptural principles.

For open-minded, progressive Catholics, these were exciting times, given the changes brought on by Pope John XXIII and Vatican Council II. For traditional Latin stalwarts clinging to the old ways, however, it must have seemed as if the Antichrist had just arrived and was hiding somewhere in St. Peter's Basilica in Rome.

Compared to Guadalupe elementary school, at Garces High, we had five classes per semester and an equal number of teachers. I found it more stimulating to be challenged by a variety of teachers as opposed to just one.

One advantage I had at Garces is that Florencio, who was already a senior when I started, had made a good name for himself for being well-behaved, good in track, and a talented pianist. Compared to me, he was also quiet. He had close to perfect attendance, was never tardy, and never went to detention. That afforded me what I'll simply refer to as "vicarious respect." I soon discovered, however, that it doesn't last long. One must stand on one's own merits.

Most of the kids in my class were from the six Bakersfield Catholic elementary schools and many of us who had played a sport would naturally join a team at Garces. So, we in those schools who had previously played a sport competing against each other, would now join as classmates and teammates at Garces. This was a little awkward given as we had been opponents before, and tempers sometimes flared. Sometimes there would be full-blown fights. At Garces, there would need to take place a forging; or rearrangement of loyalties.

The first week of school during lunch, when we were mingling in the quad, loosely comparable to a prison yard, our Guadalupe group came upon a former star from another school, Tom Bernardin. Recognizing Peter Salazar, our former quarterback, he asked,

"Hey, are you from Guadalupe?"

"Yeah. You don't like it?"

Thus, we began our integration process. To this day I do not know if Peter's response was meant as humor. The clue that it did not was in his dour expression when I commented to him that he was just being nice. But as it turned out, Peter and Tom became friends early on in the football season. In fact, we all did. We had to. Sports build loyalty.

At my first Garces football game, as a spectator, I went looking for my friends, so I climbed to the top of the bleachers. It was a warm, balmy night in September. Amid the crowd of rooting fans, I saw a girl who looked familiar standing with a friend of hers. While looking in her direction, trying to remember where I had seen her, she smiled and pointed me out to her friend. I looked around me to make sure it wasn't someone else she had taken notice of. I didn't want to look foolish, but just as I looked away, I realized I had seen her before. It was the same zany, pretty girl I'd seen twice before.

The first time I'd seen her was at Guadalupe the year before. After practice, Peter and I had gone to see how the girls were doing playing kickball against Saint Lawrence, the visiting team. I don't recall the scores or anything else other than that the girl, giggling at me now, was on the other team. To be entirely truthful, it was catching a quick glimpse of her fancy bloomers when she kicked the ball at home base that caught my attention.

The second time I saw her was at one of my brother's piano recitals that Mom dragged me to. Ever since my fiasco at the El Paso City Library I would only reluctantly go to see my brother perform. Although he was a cool and excellent performer, I would be nervous for him. It was part of the psychic bond that siblings can have.

Right at the start of the recital, held at the home of their teacher, Mrs. Shaver, I looked across the living room and saw the same pretty girl who I'd seen playing kickball. She sat there, obviously nervous, wringing her hands. I looked at her and thought, “Here’s a soul as wretchedly nervous as me,” and I felt for her.

Her name was Giovanna.

9.

During the summer between my freshman and sophomore years, I was able to witness firsthand the dire conditions of the farmworkers living in labor camps. The labor camps were usually owned and run by the growers who employed migrant farmworkers. The farmworkers stayed in the camps during the work seasons before following the various harvests northward from the Mexican border, sometimes as far as to the state of Washington.

That summer, I helped deliver Mom's *La Bonita* brand food to stores. Her Mexican food business also sold to labor camps in a thirty-mile radius, and I helped my cousin, Edmundo, deliver our products to the rural towns of Lamont, Arvin, Delano, and beyond to Old River Road in Kern County.

It was hot enough in the panel truck we drove, but I thought how much hotter it had to be for those working in the fields, with the angry sun beating down relentlessly.

There were large camps, housing hundreds of workers, and smaller camps for no more than ten to fifty. A few larger ones were clean and some even freshly painted; the clean kitchens were equipped with stainless steel tables, large stoves, and large swamp coolers. But those were rare; most were deplorable.

One of the small camps, in particular, was in essence a very dirty, old, and dilapidated house within a vineyard. Outside, under a canopy of trees, were makeshift beds made of blankets spread over wooden boards or sheets of cardboard. Spider webs on the vines surrounding the camp twinkled in the blinding sunlight. There was not even the slightest breeze, and the temperature was hovering in the high nineties.

The eating area was set up in a detached garage with dirt floors and a tiny kitchen set off to a corner. When we arrived, the cook was nowhere to be found. As we walked inside, I saw a large slab of meat that had been left on a filthy table. The putrid smell of animal fat permeated the kitchen. A large boiling pot added to the rising heat, steaming up the partially-opened windows.

I only worked in the fields one day. I was fourteen. I wanted to earn my own money independently from our family business, and so, I had persuaded my mother to allow me to tip grapes. The day came, and it did not go well. By midmorning, I had fallen way behind the crew and was quite convinced that I simply did not know how to thin the bunches, despite the quick instructions barked out to me by the "*contratista*," or labor contractor. To this day, I still don't understand how to do it. Back then, though, I thought I'd bluff it until, as if in a very bad dream, I heard someone yell out,

"Who's working this row?"

I looked behind my shoulder and saw a man walking toward me. Little surprise, it was my row he was shouting about. His image shimmered as that of a mirage rising off of a hot

country road. As he drew nearer, I whispered to myself a prolonged, "Oh, shit."

He asked whether I had ever tipped grapes before and, despite thinking how obvious the answer was, I responded, "no sir." He then asked if I was in school, and I told him that I attended Garces. At that point, his anger subsided and surprisingly he escorted me out of the "*surcos*," or rows, to an easier job.

He left me counting boxes under an umbrella. Although a bit embarrassed by his kind gesture, I swallowed my pride and survived the rest of the day. On the ride home I learned he was Giovanna's father.

At the end of the long day I went home completely exhausted. That would be the only time I worked in the fields.

The valuable instruction I received at home, at Our Lady of Guadalupe, and at Garces High, had equipped me with an intellectual understanding of social justice. As virtuous as that foundation may have been, however, it remained dormant, much like the life-sized statue of the Franciscan missionary, Padre Garcés, whose somber expression greeted all who visited our campus. After the hot San Joaquin Valley summer of 1966, my dormant conscience received a rude awakening, however, when one morning our teacher informed us that during the weekend, someone had spray-painted a red swastika on the synagogue across the street. For most of the class, the news had barely registered a mere .9 on the social-conscience Richter scale.

That Friday, I decided to visit the synagogue, Temple Beth El. I had long since stopped believing it was a mortal sin to miss Mass on Sunday, and I was stunned that a swastika would appear anywhere Mr. and Mrs. Hirschfield might have worshipped. They were Jewish, and so to me, the swastika was particularly offensive.

I don't recall much of the service, but what remains with me is the mournful voice of the congregation singing the Kaddish. Despite my inability to understand Hebrew or Aramaic, I was struck by what I felt to be a cry to God.

I was struck also by the lack of plaster and wooden statues that, for my entire childhood, I had been taught to kneel before.

After the service, Rabbi Kolatch greeted me at the door. He asked me who I was. I told him I was a student at Garces. He briefly mentioned The Friendship House out on Cottonwood Road, explaining that they helped with a tutoring program for young black kids there. I had already heard that Brother Gilbert, who I knew as a vice-principal at Garces, had been one of its organizers. I told the Rabbi I had not gone out to the Friendship House. But I did think of those nights when my friends and I had driven down to Cottonwood Road to get folks to buy us beer. After the brief encounter, I shook the Rabbi's hand and told myself I would make it a point to go visit the Friendship House.

From the moment the swastika reared its ugly head, I became more aware that life was more complex than I had ever imagined. I recalled incidents in my life and began to examine them in a different light. I remembered second grade in El Paso, Texas, when I was forced to stare at the outside wall of my school because I had spoken Spanish to my friends, and how John Shipman, when asked by my mother if we were being refused a home because we were Mexican, sheepishly replied, "yes." I remembered how Mom had requested an investigation of the Kern County Fair for putting on display a young, mentally-challenged Mexican man as "The Last of the Aztecs," and how it had turned out the carnies had bought him in Mexico to exhibit him in county fairs throughout the southwest.

Weeks after my visit to Temple Beth El, I decided to go to Cottonwood Road, only this time I went on a Saturday, alone. I took my Super-8 movie camera with me because I wanted to document the condition of Bakersfield's poor minorities. I saw it as partly redemptive, assuring myself that it made up for those beer runs. Also, my natural curiosity compelled me to seek out the dark underbelly that I had previously just accepted as normal. I saw myself as a hunter, of sorts, a young Yaqui warrior tracking dangerous game—the game in this case being evidence of poverty and racism.

That cold winter day I filmed half a dozen or so elderly, black men sitting on crates and old chairs around a bonfire. The thick ground fog concealed them within the open field in which they held counsel.

After exchanging friendly nods with me, they seemed unfazed when I entered their open lodge and began filming, no questions asked, and the friendly banter between them continued unabated. Though outside their inner circle, I felt welcomed, as among friends.

The following Monday I shared my experiences with my friend, Jean Brooks. She was a classmate and accomplished artist and poet. She drove a beige Volkswagen Beetle and had dark red hair. We shared much. Both of us felt out of place at school, having decided by our junior year that we were merely "serving time," feeling imprisoned.

It was Jean who first told me about the United Farm Workers (UFW) activities going on in Delano. Her older sister, Marcia, was a full-time volunteer with the union's newspaper, *El Malcriado*. She told me about Chris Sanchez, a photographer she'd met through Marcia, and LeRoy Chatfield, who was also a full-time volunteer with the UFW. I knew LeRoy from his time as Brother Gilbert, a member of the Christian Brothers teaching order, who had been our vice-principal at Garces High and who had hosted me for detention. Jean went on,

"You've got to meet Cesar! His hands are so small!"

She emphasized with her long delicate thumb and forefinger by holding them up to her bright brown eyes, peering through her red mane. Her excited but hushed tone sounded conspiratorial, uttered as it was in the confines of a school well-attended by the growers' progeny.

It was Jean's melodic words that breathed life into the articles I had read about Cesar Chavez and the workers he led. I knew I had to meet him.

10.

By my junior year at Garces, Giovanna had become one of "them," a grower's daughter. I was now a known UFW sympathizer and a friend of Jean, who proudly wore her farmworker movement buttons to school. Given the contentious nature of the farm labor struggle, the rift that had already existed between us became a wide chasm across which even the familiarity of childhood couldn't span. The lesson I was about to learn was that blood runs as thick for Italian growers as it does for Mexican laborers and sympathizers. Both Catholic, perhaps, but worshipping at different altars.

Brother Kenneth, our civics teacher, assigned a final project. I decided mine would be about Cesar's first major fast for the farmworkers' movement. I had heard from Jean that Cesar had begun the fast as a means of affirming his principles of non-violence. A daily Mass was being offered in the co-op service station building at the movement's Forty Acres property near Delano, on Garces Highway. By the time I learned of it, Cesar was about halfway through his twenty-five-day fast.

The following Saturday, I drove to Delano to attend the Mass and experience in-person the phenomenon known as the farmworkers' movement.

When I arrived, the co-op was already packed. A simple altar in the adobe-brick rectangular room stood at the north wall. Priests were ready and waiting for Cesar, who had not yet entered from the tiny room in the back where he was temporarily living.

Years later, Cesar told me how a contingency of farmworkers barged into this room one afternoon. In good faith, they had traveled down to Delano to convince him to break his fast with, of all things, chorizo burritos. Smiling incredulously, the now nationally- known vegetarian humorously described those devoted followers as the "Burrito Posse." It would have been an assault with a deadly burrito for a devoted vegetarian undergoing a long fast.

As I made my way further into the room, the scent of people, flowers, and burning candles called to mind my altar boy days at Our Lady of Guadalupe. Except here, the officiating priest wore the regular white toga, but with a colorful Mexican *sarape* draped over him. He was flanked by two other priests, similarly dressed.

As the congregation sang a Spanish hymn, I looked around the room for Cesar, and moments later he entered from a narrow hallway. On each side of him, were two large men who appeared to be assistants. One could see the fast had taken its toll. He took slow, deliberate steps as he surveyed the people in attendance. At times, he grimaced and was unsteady on his feet. He was assisted as he made his way past his followers to the front of the humble but brightly decorated altar.

I became acutely aware that I was witnessing something very different from any other Mass I had ever seen. This one was, in a strange inexplicable way, a much more powerful ceremony, being both spiritual and political; that was the magic!

Cesar embodied a movement and stood in its midst as the eye of a powerful storm. To his followers, he was the brave warrior fighting injustice, not only in the fields, but everywhere our people were scourged by discrimination and sub-human conditions. In my view, Cesar had by his dedication and sacrifice, proven himself to be the leader to follow.

After a couple of weeks had gone by, I returned to Delano for the end of Cesar's fast. It was to be the first of the three major hunger strikes in his life. I packed my camera, tape recorder, and notebooks and drove thirty miles to Delano where I got a room.

The next morning, I was up at the crack of dawn, ready to beat the crowds and set up my tripod at the Delano Park where the Mass with Cesar would take place. Bobby Kennedy would be joining Cesar in receiving the Eucharist, along with thousands of farmworkers and supporters.

By official estimates, there were over five thousand people who attended the event. Although I arrived early, access was very tight. Nevertheless, I managed to get a few shots by pushing my way through the crowd or climbing a tree for the better shots. Still, I could not get close enough and at the end was not satisfied.

When the ceremony ended, I thought there might be a way I could get good footage of Senator Kennedy, but it had to be when he left the park. The way I planned to manage that was by getting near the pathway leading to his vehicles. It worked, and in a few minutes, I saw the Senator's entourage walking in my direction. I immediately pulled out my camera from my waist and began filming.

When he came within ten feet of me, I heard him call out, "You have been very busy this morning!"

"Yes, I have, Mr. Senator!" I called back. We exchanged smiles as he continued walking.

On June 6, 1968, the Senator was assassinated at the Ambassador Hotel in Los Angeles after giving his California primary victory speech. It was less than ninety days after sharing the Eucharist with Cesar in Delano.

I found out in my senior year that throughout most of the time at

Garces High, Brother Daniel, our principal, and others at the school had tried to find out why it was that I was usually surrounded by other boys. They wondered what it was that I could be telling them. Mom revealed to me that in a telephone conference with our school principal the year before, he'd informed her that they'd resorted to eavesdropping to find out. Although I was put off by what I saw as an invasion of my privacy, I was not in the least concerned given as there was nothing subversive or abnormal about our interactions. All of it was simply normal talk, with some off-color humor at times. I wonder now if they were concerned I was organizing for the UFW at school.

All during my senior year I had taken to devouring college catalogs, now a thing of the past, to help me gauge what each college offered, to figure out what studies I would focus on, and, ultimately, what college I would attend. My head was spinning with so much information that by the time of my graduation I did not have a clear idea of which schools I wanted to get in.

As I saw it then, my two career path choices were as follows: becoming a Navy pilot and serving in Vietnam or becoming a lawyer. The thought of becoming a movement or union lawyer had not yet struck me. I had not been politicized enough. That would happen two years later.

"But, for now, relax," I told myself and decided to enjoy the rest of the school year. I had by then contracted a serious case of senioritis.

Before the graduation ceremony, I approached David Romero, Mike Doyle, and Tim Conley with a plan to go fishing immediately after the graduation party, which was to be held at the Hill House Motel. It was a bit crazy as I was never into fishing, but now that I look back on it, I am certain it had more to do with spending a few more hours together with my friends before we went our separate ways.

They all agreed, thinking I would not hold them to it. The plan was simple: I would drive and we would each take our rods, plus beer and snacks.

The ceremony was quite impressive, with our class singing the song from *The Man Of La Mancha,* "The Impossible Dream."

For me, the highlight of the evening was when Lucía Ajénjo, an exchange student from Santander, Spain who I had dated during my senior year, came up to me after the ceremony with flowers in hand and congratulated me with a warm hug. That summer Lucía returned to her home in Santander, and we would never see each other again. I did send her carnations for her birthday, and we wrote for about three months thereafter.

After the graduation party at the Hill House had ended, I got a cup of coffee and we were off to the Kern River, which snakes its way down from Lake Isabella to Bakersfield.

We were all packed in the car and Mike and I, the two least groggy, were in the front with me at the wheel. At 3:30 a.m., we drove into the dark.

Making our way up the canyon, I rolled down my window to see if the cold would rouse the troops. But they merely complained about how cold it was, so I rolled it back up and focused back on the huge rocks we were approaching and the jagged cliffs leading to the riverbed below. The wind whipped up.

After engaging the sharp turns for some time, I found an area that I liked for greeting the sun, which would soon be rising above the surrounding peaks.

When it did rise, however, everyone grudgingly got out of the car, and it became clear to me that this was a bad idea. We were all in good spirits, but we were just too exhausted and too accustomed to the comforts of our own beds.

After a quick vote, we were all back in the car and heading back home. Majority carried.

The narrow two-lane canyon road had many twists and turns, but after a few miles there came a long, straight incline. Within minutes of when we left, I had lost even my co-pilot, Mike, who was now clearly asleep, snoring. I turned off the heater as even on low it was starting to make me groggy.

The radio did not help, as the oldies transported me elsewhere, *"helplessly... going under..."*

"MARCO! LOOK OUT!"

A delivery truck going well beyond the speed limit was coming right at us. It seemed like it all happened in slow motion as I swerved back into my lane.

An accident was narrowly averted, and though I'd like to believe it was fate or Mike's sixth sense, I'll never know for sure. Nevertheless, we were all thankful to him for saving the day. Something woke him up.

Twelve years later I experienced the same slowing of time while traveling with Cesar to Los Angeles on Highway 14 through Mojave. Going at eighty miles per hour, two of the tires blew out. Cesar, from the beginning of the spinout, calmly gave his driver, David Valles, instructions on how to correct the vehicle until it came to a complete and safe stop off the roadway. Cesar's investigation later revealed that two of the brand-new tires had been slashed within hours before our trip to see the movie, *Zoot Suit,* in Los Angeles. When it was over, I thought back to my friends and myself on that narrow Kern River Canyon road.

After graduating from Garces High, I never returned to retrieve my Super-8 movie that I had submitted along with my written report of that historic day in Delano. On my fortieth high school reunion I saw Brother Kenneth, and I asked him if he knew what happened to them. He had left the Christian Brothers many years earlier, and he recalled leaving it at the home the brothers shared on the campus. He told me there were no longer any religious teachers at Garces. "It's gone, then," I said to him, resigned over my loss.

When I began writing this book, I researched the Farmworkers Movement Documentation Project created by LeRoy Chatfield. It is now managed by U.C. San Diego. One day, while going through dozens of photographs in that collection, I got to one that froze me. In it, I saw myself at the age of eighteen on that day in 1968 in Delano. I am wearing my signature, brown, corduroy sports coat and carrying my Super-8 camera at that fleeting moment with Senator Robert Kennedy.

PART TWO

11.

A lot of changes had taken place at home by the time I reached my senior year at Garces. Mom had remarried and given birth to the daughter she had always wanted, Patricia. For Florencio and I, it was a win-win. Our baby sister brought joy to our home and made Mom very happy. Her father, Mauricio Talamantes, became involved in the business and also became good friends with my cousin, Edmundo. The marriage only lasted five years, probably due to their age difference and Mom's strong will that she developed from running a business on her own. "I wasn't this way before, *hijo*. Life, and having to fend for you two boys alone, made me this way."

I attended Bakersfield Community College for two years after graduating from Garces High. My brother transferred to California State College at Northridge as a music major. In the summer of 1970, after completing my last year of community college, I went to Los Angeles (LA) as a volunteer for the UFW grape boycott. The boycott was intended to put economic pressure on the grape growers to sign union contracts with their workers. I volunteered under the direction of LeRoy Chatfield. Co-directing the LA boycott was Chris Hartmire, founder-director of the Migrant Ministry, a grassroots organization and strong ally of the Union.

Before leaving for LA, I decided to apply to San Jose State for my junior and senior years of college, mainly because of its student politics. For one, in 1968 I had seen track stars and alumni Harry Edwards, John Carlos, and Tommie Smith protest at the Mexico City Olympics. Their black-gloved fists in the air were a civil rights gesture never before seen in our country. It captured my imagination as well as that of millions of others around the world. Also, a couple of Army veterans from Our Lady of Guadalupe, Ramon Martinez and Pat Alderette told me about their walkout from the San Jose State commencement the same year. Hearing it first-hand from them clinched it for me. I applied and I was accepted.

Among my Bakersfield friends who joined in volunteering for the LA boycott was Mary Fuentes, who knew me from Garces High and Bakersfield College. She saw me as a political mentor, and I looked upon her as a kid sister. Her parents, Otilia and Armando, had met while they were farmworkers, and like her parents, she was "*de puro hueso colorado*"— a staunch supporter. Once in LA, Mary was assigned to work in the Santa Ana boycott office, and so, we only got the chance to say hello on Saturdays at our weekly meetings at Loyola Marymount College in LA. Due to budgetary reasons, the amount of personal phone calls we could make was very limited, so socializing at these meetings was as spirited as a Baptist revival.

I was assigned to live in a stately house on Olympic Boulevard. It was at least eighty years old and weathered, sitting at the top of a steep hill, with two sturdy palm trees flanking the wide, twenty-foot-long sidewalk that led up to it. The house had been rented at a discount by the UFW to house its East LA volunteers.

Those assigned to live at the Olympic boycott house were a good mix; myself and Louie, both Chicanos from Bakersfield; Robert, a very big and friendly Native-American from Tolleson, Arizona; and David, a Jewish Yale graduate and heady intellectual from back east. Then there was Bobby, a farmworker who was the grandson of dust-bowlers that had migrated to California; an "Okie," as he proudly called himself. Bobby had boycott-seniority over us and was therefore in charge overall of our house.

We were each given a supermarket as our responsibility in an area starting from Boyle Heights, East Los Angeles, and further east. My assigned store was in the San Gabriel Valley, where the smog was thickest.

It was our mission as representatives to educate customers on UFW history and about the living and working conditions of farmworkers in California and to convince them to stop shopping at or boycott a certain store until the management agreed to stop carrying non-union grapes. Our job required an intuitive knowledge of human behavior, persuasiveness, and a sincere and friendly attitude. We also handed out UFW literature to whoever accepted it. In the evenings, we returned to the house on Olympic and while preparing dinner, we would work on our reports; i.e. the data on how many customer contacts we made, who was receptive or hostile, and who might be interested in volunteering. When LeRoy called, we were each also expected to offer any insights we might have on honing our techniques, as well as discussing any concerns or questions we were asked by the customers during our time in the field canvassing.

After a quick, visual assessment of our target shoppers, the most important rule was to not waste time arguing with hostile people and to tailor our approach to each individual. For example, if we saw a customer with children, we focused on issues of child labor in the fields; if the person was elderly, we would focus on the fact that farmworkers did not have retirement benefits and therefore, were required to work well into their "golden years."

The most powerful issue was the growers' use of toxic, unregulated pesticides in the fields, poisoning consumers and workers alike. The UFW had a lot of credibility and good faith in the bank of public opinion, and the public knew that we were at the forefront of protecting consumers, as well as farmworkers, from pesticides in this country. As Cesar liked to say, "it's a double-whammy."

We all had stories about our favorite "turn-aways" which we shared with each other and our friends. A turn-away is when one convinces a former shopper to become a boycotter by refusing to shop at a store carrying non-union grapes. My time for a turn-away came outside a Lucky Store assigned to me in San Gabriel. It happened at the end of an extremely hot day. A well-dressed woman, approximately ten years my senior, approached the store. The closer she got to me, the more concerned she looked. But before she could look away from me, I reached out and gave her a flier.

Just as I began telling her about the fight in the fields for better pay and working conditions, the manager came out of the store and walked directly toward us.

"Good morning, Mrs. Snyder. How are you?"

"I'm doing fine, thank you," she replied.

The manager looked at me with a dirty look on his face and asked her, "Is this man bothering you in any way?"

"No. He's telling me about the farmworkers and the horrible conditions they live and work in."

I turned to Mrs. Snyder, disregarded the manager, and continued telling her how farmworkers were excluded from the National Labor Relations Act and how they were exercising their right to expose this injustice to the public with a boycott. I noticed the manager kept glaring at me, so I directed my comments to him as well. His face began to turn red as he became visibly livid. A dark reddish hue rose from his neck to his jaws.

"Mrs. Snyder, you have the right to go about your business undisturbed," he said. "Let me walk you into the store. It's clear this man is harassing you."

"No, he's not bothering me at all."

She and I exchanged smiles, and she then looked straight at the manager and told him, "Bill, I'm sorry, but I just can't shop here." She took the flier, walked to her car, and drove away without looking back.

The manager returned to his store and called the police, reporting me for "disturbing the peace." When the police arrived, however, after they had spoken to the manager, I told them exactly what happened, and the sergeant refused to even give me a warning. When he informed me that the manager had insisted that they make a citizen's arrest, it made the turn-away all the sweeter.

That evening LeRoy was pleased to hear my report and told me the manager had called him complaining about me bothering his customers. LeRoy backed me up all the way and at our next meeting at Loyola, he spoke about the incident to the entire group of more than two-hundred boycotters.

It was small victories such as these that made the sweat and grind worthwhile.

The hot, muggy summer, heavy smog, and long days were taking a toll on everyone, but our spirits remained high. Great strides were being made in every major city in the US and Canada, and they were being reported to us by LeRoy and Chris at our highly-spirited weekly meetings. That helped our resolve greatly, as we were becoming more and more convinced that victory was not far off. Those of us based at the Olympic house, however, were beginning to get a little too undisciplined, not as far as our work was concerned, but in how we unwound at the end of the day. Usually, LeRoy called us in the early evening, but on one Friday evening he didn't call until after 8:00 p.m. By then, we were well into our happy hour.

We had stocked up on enough beer for the weekend, which was flowing quicker than usual. By the time LeRoy called, we were all quite buzzed. Because of my long history with him, which the others were aware of, I was given the privilege of speaking with him first.

"Hi, Marco. How was your day?"

"It was good!" was all I could summon, feeling a bit embarrassed about being caught drinking.

I motioned to the others to shut up, but then they started their antics, mimicking me, trying to make me lose it. When speaking with LeRoy, I still thought of him as Brother Gilbert from Garces, whom I would be sent to for detention, so there was still that fear and respect factor.

I was starting to dread the conversation.

"Marco? What's going on?"

"Sorry LeRoy, just relaxing here."

"Are you drinking?"

"Drinking?"

That immediately got the others' collective attention. They all motioned desperately to say "no!"

"Yes. We're having a little beer," was my delayed response.

I tried to quickly change the subject by giving him my report, but the only phone in the house was in the kitchen where the keg was. It was becoming more difficult to keep my colleagues quiet.

"Okay. Let me speak with Bobby."

I handed the phone to Bobby, thinking he was the best person to explain. Bobby had been on the boycott for over two years, and if anyone had a "get out of jail free card" for us, it was him.

The following week I was transferred to what I jokingly referred to as the "Siberia" of the LA boycott—Irwindale, California. At this time, construction of the 210 Freeway had just begun and huge rock quarries running alongside the foothills were a known attraction, making for incessant and noisy traffic. The housing was in a small rectory off to the side of an old Catholic mission. For the rest of the summer, I would be rooming there with Pat Bonner, a friendly, though quiet, Jesuit. The entire structure was made of gray river stones, enclosed by a stone wall. It was in Irwindale that I would be introduced to soft processed cheese. Pat had a reputation for thriving on it, so we got lots of it from the donations center.

I knew my party days in LA were over. "*Por la causa, brother!*" my friend Robert from Arizona kidded me, "For the cause!"

12.

At our boycott update meeting at Loyola in late July, Chris and LeRoy announced that all of the Delano grape growers had reached an agreement with the United Farm Workers Organizing Committee (UFWOC) covering the entire table grape industry. In all, this represented twenty-nine companies whose workers would be covered by union contracts with wage increases, benefits, and protections from mistreatment. This victory came after five years of striking and boycotting, which had begun in 1965.

The signing of the collective bargaining agreements was to take place at the Forty Acres in Delano. Busloads of us from LA were invited to attend. I was one of those chosen, which frankly made me feel honored, yet unworthy. I felt my sacrifice paled in comparison to that of many others, workers and supporters, who had sacrificed much more than I had, for many years before me.

As I drove those last thirty miles from Bakersfield to Delano, I recalled the trip I had made there in 1968, when I went to document the end of Cesar's fast for my school project. So many things had followed since then. But one really stood out at the moment. After that historic day at Delano Park, Ernest Pierucci, our student body president, recruited me to work as a volunteer on the Kern County

Kennedy Campaign, run by local attorney, Timothy Lemucci. For a brief time, I helped in the Senator's presidential campaign, canvassing in Bakersfield. After his assassination, a dark cloud hung over me for years when it came to politics, and any political ambitions I may have had were buried that summer of '68.

Cesar's sacrifice of fasting for twenty-five days had paid off, too, as had the sacrifices of so many others in the movement. Millions of Americans had come around to supporting our boycott. The many sacrifices the grape strikers had endured was the point of the speech Cesar gave in that packed UFW hiring hall. I distinctly recall how all the growers shuffled into the hall, looking crestfallen, as if on their way to the gallows; everyone that is, except for both John Giumarra Junior and Senior, who had led the growers to the negotiating table. Unlike the others, they were beaming with assuredness, even engaging Jerry Cohen, the UFW's general counsel who had been part of the negotiations, in friendly banter. It was hard to imagine they had all been enemies for so long, but with the agreements, the grape boycott would end, and the growers could once more sell their grapes, but only with the UFW-eagle emblem prominently stamped on their boxes.

Unfortunately, the partnership between the Union and the grape growers would deteriorate before the three-year terms of the contracts ended in 1973.

After the twenty-nine growers signed, Cesar, clad in a brilliant barong shirt, told those present, including a large national press, how ninety-five percent of the strikers had lost their homes and cars during their long struggle. He emphasized how their sacrifice had proven to the world that, through nonviolent action, justice is attainable.

Speaking on behalf of the growers, John Giumarra, Jr. remarked how he hoped that from "this new foundation" the Union could "move on to greater things."

Though we had good reason to celebrate, the next day we had to be in Salinas where the stage was being set for yet another long battle, this time with the even more powerful lettuce and row crop industry of the Salinas Valley and its ally, the Teamsters Union.

The UFW board and staff were up to the challenge, however, with our opponents clearly in our sights. As the grape contracts were being signed, UFW attorney Bill Carder was already in Salinas taking witness statements and preparing an antitrust lawsuit against the Salinas Valley growers that ultimately led the Teamsters, in 1977, to sign a jurisdictional pact agreement to respect the rights of the UFW to organize farmworkers. The gist of the lawsuit was that the signing of "backdoor" contract agreements, without worker consent, violated the California Labor Code.

Once again, but on a different front, the Union was about to engage in another epic fight. This time it would be covered by the Bay Area press, notoriously comprised of progressive-liberal journalists eager to cover the fight in Steinbeck country.

Before the historic grape contract signing, LeRoy let me know that I would be traveling with him and a handful of others to the Salinas Valley immediately afterward. Our mission was to organize one of four marches that would come together at a rally at Hartnell College in Salinas. We had five days to make this happen.

My mother offered to lend me the new Ford station wagon she had bought for the bakery. It was a way for her to help the movement, but she was also concerned that without it I might not make it to San Jose State in the fall to start my junior year. I accepted and promised her I would be in San Jose in September.

The marches were to protest the recent contracts between the vegetable growers and the Teamsters, who had been wooed into a conspiracy by the row-crop industry, who were fearful of a Delano-type victory in Salinas.

After a brief celebration in Delano, I drove most of the night north to Greenfield, California where I stayed with a family of UFW supporters. On the way into the Salinas Valley, I passed lush green fields being tended to by a highly-organized workforce.

Each company had its distinctive trademark colors and logos painted on to its pickup trucks, tractor-trailers, and buses. It was like looking inside a finely-made Swiss watch; all the different parts, though distinct, were all working in precise coordination.

Despite my purpose for being in the Salinas Valley, I couldn't help but admire this perfectly choreographed display of company forces.

Cesar said, "We're in for a good, long fight."

The UFW's temporary headquarters in Salinas were located in a small, storefront office on East Alisal Street. Marshall Ganz, who was one of the UFW Executive Board members, and the other organizers from this office were planning a large rally in Watsonville on July 31 and then a four-day march culminating in another rally at Hartnell College. Marshall, who had been a freedom-fighter in the South with the Student Non-Violent Coordinating Committee (SNCC), I remembered from when he went to visit Brother Gilbert at Garces High. It was following the school year of 1967 that Brother Gilbert joined the Union and assumed his birth name—LeRoy Chatfield.

In our first meeting, LeRoy laid out the general plan for the Greenfield to Salinas branch of the march and how we would coordinate with the other marches coming from Watsonville, Gilroy, and Hollister.

Four years later, in 1975, LeRoy became one of the first five members appointed to the Agricultural Labor Relations Board by Governor Jerry Brown. I worked for him during some of that time. He described himself to me then as being "laconic," which made me smile. I did so because, being true to his word, he had condensed his character traits to that one irreducible, self-descriptive term, so it had always boggled my mind how someone of so few words could be such an effective organizer.

One of his methods was to bring you in the loop by providing you with the "dots," while standing back, then motivating you to connect them all yourself. It was both simple and engaging, and it also instilled a sense of proprietorship in the project.

One of my suggestions on that first evening was to lead the march with a life-size wooden cross, at the top of which would be nailed a crown of braided, barbed wire. It was nothing very original, but it quickly captured the imagination of two young farmworkers who were immediately assigned to the project.

One woman pointed out how the cross might help galvanize the Salinas Valley workers, who, she emphatically made clear, were not as militant as those in Delano.

By the next morning, we had our rustic cross. It was about seven feet in height and constructed of weathered lumber. The crown of rusted barbed wire was nailed to the top, and the names of the towns along the route were painted on it. After the meeting, LeRoy asked that I go with him to see some people.

"We still have some loose ends for tomorrow," he explained.

On our way to some of the labor camps, LeRoy made a stop at the rectory of the only Catholic church in town, Holy Trinity.

"Marco, would you please go and ask the priest if we can use the church hall? We have some marchers who will need a place to stay. Oh, yes, assure him we'll make sure to clean up."

Despite being caught a bit by surprise and feeling a little awkward about asking, I stepped out of the car and walked up the long walkway through a well-manicured lawn and garden.

I knocked and waited. When the door opened, behind the gate, I saw only a dark figure silhouetted by dim lighting from inside.

"Good morning Father, my name is Marco Lopez and I'm a volunteer for the United Farmworkers. My reason . . ."

SLAM!

I walked all the way back down to the car, feeling both stunned and dejected. "Gee, LeRoy, he must have used both hands to shut that door!"

"What did you tell him?" LeRoy reminded me of Clint Eastwood, soft voice and furrowed forehead.

I gave him a look, and he smiled while I busted out laughing. LeRoy, I strongly suspected, was trying to teach me a lesson. I was certain of it, but I didn't know exactly what or why. And sure enough, as we drove away from Holy Trinity, he admitted to having called the rectory before driving out with me. The priest had mumbled something to him before hanging up.

"I thought a fresh voice might make a difference," he said. "Marco, some people just claim to be Christian, but aren't. They're 'unchristian,'" is how he laconically summed it up.

Every night of the four-day march from Greenfield to Salinas, there was a town hall meeting to alert, inform, and recruit the workers for the next day, as well as for the final march into Salinas. Given that not all of the people who would speak at the meetings were Spanish-speaking, I was asked by LeRoy to act as an interpreter. When I was a child, I often translated television programs and movies for my grandmother, Domitila, on her visits to Bakersfield, so this was second nature.

Now, I just had to supplement my vocabulary. The evening meeting, in a Masonic Hall in Gonzales, was packed with a fever-pitched crowd. This meeting was to be our last push into Salinas the next day. Our seven-foot-tall cross was displayed in the center of the stage.

LeRoy, who spoke admirable Spanish, opened the meeting.

After warming up the workers, he called on Jerry Cohen, the Union's general counsel, to be the last speaker. I was nervous, him being a lawyer and all. He got right into it and I thought, "this guy's going too fast!" I managed to keep up only by interrupting him whenever I thought he'd said a digestible portion. The Q & A went smoothly so that by the end of his talk, he and I were in perfect synch. After the meeting, LeRoy told me Cohen had asked him, "Hey, where did you find this guy?"

LeRoy added that Cohen thought I might have embellished, but had done it quite well, judging by the applause he got. I was impressed by him as well, and it was then that the idea of someday working with him in the UFW legal department started taking root.

In my defense, I explained to LeRoy that generally any idea, thought, or concept expressed in Spanish requires, on the average, more words than when said in English.

What I didn't know then was that Spanish is *"la lengua de los ángeles"* (the tongue of angels). I was to learn that from Cesar the next day, before he addressed the multitude of workers.

The march into Salinas was jubilant, and the number of marchers was in the thousands. Black and red UFW flags waved in all directions throughout the city's streets, which, for those few hours, we owned. Then the rally began.

Now was the time for Cesar and Dolores Huerta to lay it out—to unequivocally express to the growers and Teamsters that they were not only accepting their challenge, but that it was going to be a fight to the end.

Dolores came next in the order of speakers. Dolores had worked side by side with Cesar organizing the UFW from its earliest days and was the union's First Vice-President. She was born in the same town as my mother, Dawson, New Mexico, so like myself she came from a family of miners who had migrated to California. To me, she was the most fiery and fearless. She was also not as much the diplomat, never being one to use veneers and always wearing her heart on her sleeve. She was exceptionally loyal to Cesar but remained fiercely independent. Being the less measured of the two, Dolores tended to rely on raw intuition and energy, and, if necessary, throwing caution to the wind. Her swashbuckler attitude gave her the ability to embolden the women, while also challenging the men to lay it all on the line for *La Causa* (The Cause).

"*¿Tenemos miedo*?! (Are we afraid?!) Dolores called out.

"*No!*" the crowd responded.

"*¿Tenemos miedo?!* (Are we afraid?!) She repeated.

"*No!*" The crowd echoed.

"*¿Tienen miedo*?! (Are *you* afraid?!) She challenged the crowd.

"*NO!*" was the roaring, drawn-out response.

Dolores was our dragon-slayer and fear was the dragon.

When Cesar began to speak, he apologized to the workers for having to speak in English first, explaining how it was necessary because of the press deadlines. But then he added, much to the delight of the workers, that he would then address them "*en la lengua de los* ángeles" (in the tongue of angels.)

After speaking to the press for approximately twenty minutes, Cesar once again turned his full attention back to the workers. His address to them was more personal, utilizing a masterful blend of modulation of pitches and body gestures, enhancing comprehension as well as connecting himself to the workers.

At the high points of his speech, Cesar's body pitched slightly forward with his index finger pointing upward—not unlike a prophet of old.

By the end of his speech, he had painstakingly laid the foundation and framework for this new campaign, against new obstacles, confident that the struggle would continue.

He closed the rally with, "*Viva la huelga*!" (Long live the strike!)

The rally closed with a *Huelga* applause in perfect unison, increasingly louder and faster to the end.

It was truly spellbinding. In all, more than 5,000 marchers from Greenfield, Gilroy, Hollister, and Watsonville converged in Salinas on that Sunday, August 2, 1970, and Dolores and Cesar nailed it.

It all contrasted with the lightning, silently flashing in the dark sky over the distant fields.

13.

The morning after the Salinas rally, I headed back home to organize my move from Bakersfield to San Jose. I had decided that after graduating from college in two years, I would immediately move on to law school, so I feared that any delay might derail my plans. But before leaving for northern California, I planned to march in the National Chicano Moratorium of August 29, 1970.

The concept for the Moratorium arose from a cadre of Chicanos who realized, despite the government propaganda that victory in the Vietnam War was near, the mounting casualties in the war were disproportionately affecting the Chicano population. It was undeniably clear that Latinos and the young poor of the country were the principal fodder for the military-industrial complex in what was an illegal and unjust war. And yet it continued, interminably.

Officially, the Chicano activists had proclaimed, "Our struggle is not in Vietnam but in the movement for social justice at home." It was for that reason that I decided to march with them.

One of the voices critical of police brutality and the Vietnam war was that of Ruben Salazar, a naturalized US citizen and investigative journalist originally from Chihuahua, Mexico. As early as 1963, when he began writing for the LA Times, he focused on covering the Mexican-

American community. At times, Salazar cited the US-Mexico Treaty of Guadalupe Hidalgo (1848) which ended the war perpetrated against Mexico, as a source of protection against the injustices heaped upon it. Although under modern international law this "agreement" would be null and void because it was signed under compulsion with US troops in Mexico, it did, on its surface at least, grant Mexican citizens living in the conquered territories certain civil rights and protections. It's of little wonder then that Professor Richard Griswold del Castillo has referred to the Treaty as a "legacy of conflict."

Because Salazar exposed these issues, he was shadowed by the FBI (Federal Bureau of Investigation) up to the day he was assassinated. The reason they gave for their interest in him is that he was suspected of being a communist, but it was a false pretense.

In a PBS documentary about him, he was profiled as "the man in the middle," and that, I assure you, he was.

On the morning of the Moratorium, I left for Los Angeles with John Gonzalez, the younger brother of my friend, Ruben, who was serving in Vietnam as military police, an MP. I hoped that the adventure might shape his own views on the war, and John seemed open-minded, which is all one can ask.

As we climbed the Grapevine, I asked him, "Did Ruben ever tell you how, or why he enlisted?"

John furrowed his forehead and eyebrows, then responded as if in deep thought, "Not really. No, except that he thought he might have more input as to where he would serve."

I intended to dispel any thoughts John might have that Ruben had joined out of pure patriotism, without minimizing Ruben's contribution to his country. I thought Ruben's story was a poignant story, exciting at first, even funny, then ending with the awakening to its serious consequences.

Ruben and I were both at Bakersfield College the day the results of the draft lottery were announced in 1970. We drove to school early and did exactly as we had planned the day before: I bought us each a cup of coffee; Ruben bought the *Bakersfield Californian*. We took our coffee to the yard, sat down on the ground, and Ruben opened up the paper. The lottery was based on one's birthday, so we began searching for our respective birthdates. No sooner had Ruben started down the list that I sensed he had stopped.

"Hey Ruben, what's the matter?" I asked, though I could see it on his face.

"Shit. I'm screwed."

"Where are you?"

"Fucking number three."

He was stunned. We both knew he was certain to be drafted. I continued reading on to the next page where I finally saw my birthday buried in the last column at number 263.

The die was cast and, as fate would have it, two close childhood friends would soon be separated by war.

"I'm going to enlist," Ruben said.

"Why?" I asked.

"It'll give me a better chance of choosing my assignment."

I doubted it. I never told him that with his enlistment he would become government property. I just figured he knew that and did not want to make his misery worse.

John became visibly upset after I finished telling him his brother's story, so I told him, "Don't get me wrong, John. Ruben is as patriotic as you and me, but deep down inside I know he didn't want to end up in Vietnam."

It had been a clear day driving up the Grapevine into Los Angeles. That day the Grateful Dead were playing at "The Club" on LA's west side. It was all over the radio. But in East Los Angeles, most of the young were focused on the Moratorium.

I gassed up in East LA, and then we ate signature burritos made by John's Mom on our way to the park where the march was to start.

We were driving on Whittier Boulevard into East LA when I sensed a mixed festivity and uneasiness in the air. We were both looking forward to the march, and from his mood, I could tell my preparations had eased his anxieties. But now, he would have to embark on his own quest as far as the war and his conscience were concerned.

By the time we had parked and made the trek to the staging area of the march, there were already hundreds of people, organized by their respective organizations. Flags, banners, and bullhorns added to the excitement. There were families, teenagers, and military veterans, many of whom were older Mexican-American vets from prior wars who came in uniform, with Raza movement and farmworker buttons alongside their military decorations. Musicians tuned their instruments and warmed up groups of marchers. There were many signs and flags of both the US and Mexico and some black and red UFW banners and flags as well.

It was announced that the march would be starting soon, and so John and I found a space and waited. We would later learn that we were close to 30,000 in number, far beyond the approximately 5,000 in the Salinas march. Personally, it was a coalescing of the same principle of justice through non-violence in both our urban and rural struggles.

Each march takes on a life of its own, based on the location, subject, leadership, and the people who join in its numbers. This was a youthful march led by young leaders wanting to add their voice to the national anti-war movement. They had witnessed the death of four Kent State students, killed by the overreaction of the Ohio National Guard, barely four months earlier.

But ours was to be a strictly non-violent march and fully protected by the First Amendment, so what could go wrong? One could have reasonably believed that there would be no martyrs in East Los Angeles on that day.

We began in high spirits, passing through residential as well as business or mixed neighborhoods. It was a warm day and some neighborly people offered the marchers water. At the midpoint, I noticed an increasing number of marchers buying refreshments at businesses we passed. A small number of onlookers drank beer.

As we got nearer to our destination, the line formation started to break up, and the marchers filled the entire street. But still the order was kept by the monitors who carried bullhorns for leading chants and safety directives.

There were "*porras,*" or anti-war chants, yelled out by groups or individuals.

"*Chále con sú guerra!*" (The hell with your war!)

"Hell no, we won't go!"

"Bring our brothers home!

In the small downtown area of East LA, the street, flanked by multi-story buildings, echoed with the crescendo of chants and songs. The increasing sound level caused a marked increase in the march's energy level. John and I glanced at each other with broad smiles of incredulity. We were a long way from conservative, complacent Bakersfield.

As we marched to Laguna Park, where a rally was to take place, people were joining in droves. Some were recruited by marchers along the way, and we all cheered when individuals or small groups would join us, impromptu.

Seeing as we were near the park, I warned John that we should stay close as it would be impossible to find one another if we got separated. He let out a nervous laugh, and I reiterated what I'd said with an exaggerated, arched eyebrow that drew a smile from him. Being circumspect of large crowds, as well as of the herd mentality, I guided us to the opposite side of the park, instead of following the monitors' direction to fill the area toward the front of the stage. We stood there watching the rest of the marchers go by.

At the nearest intersection to us, South Alma Avenue and Whittier Boulevard, was a corner liquor store doing brisk business selling water, sodas, and beer. We remained in place but soon the crowd swelled to fill the entire park. The march leaders began to take the stage.

The master of ceremonies gave his introductory remarks, asking the people in the peripheries to draw in closer to allow space for others still arriving.

The rally had barely begun, when from the corner across from the liquor store, I heard some commotion coming from what appeared to be some local homeboys hanging around, some carrying quarts of beer and taking swigs as they meandered toward Laguna Park.

Coming down South Alma Avenue, the narrower side street that ran up from the liquor store, were numerous Los Angeles Sheriff SWAT team members. Their boots, marching in synch, thundered as the cadence of a rushing force. They were in formation, holding their large riot batons out in front of them.

As soon as the SWAT teams arrived at the intersection, without me seeing exactly what started the riot, all hell broke loose between the homeboys, or provocateurs, and the baton-wielding sheriff deputies. Bottles flew at the deputies who charged at them. At first, the homeboys were holding their own, but as more deputies made their way to the intersection, they retreated into the park.

A helicopter appeared, circling low above the park. Tear gas began raining down on all of us peaceful protestors. People ran about in confusion, rubbing their eyes and some splashing their faces with water, without being able to take shelter.

Some people in the group attempted to stop the deputies from their rear attacks. The batons, however, came down on the defenseless who could only use their hands and arms to shield themselves. The sound of mahogany crashing down on human bones would politicize me even further.

I called out for John who I had lost track of. I had last seen him starting to back away from the park heading toward the street across from it, but he was now nowhere in sight. I, too, fled the park walking in the general direction of where I had parked the car, stopping only briefly to ask an elderly couple sitting outside their small house if I could use their water hose.

"*Si, pásele,*" (Yes, come in) said the man, with a look of concern in his deep-set eyes.

I opened their gate and made my way into the yard to wash the tear gas out of my eyes, face, and hair then left after thanking the couple who were still sitting on their small porch. They smiled behind the camouflage provided by their garden.

I continued walking and soon regained my bearings toward the car. A few blocks further I turned left onto a wider street. I saw many police vehicles from different agencies speeding to Laguna Park. I was comforted only by the thought that I was headed away from what was by now a full-blown riot. The swarm of police and news helicopters above told the story.

My thoughts turned to John, who I hoped would be waiting at the car.

From about fifty yards away, I spotted a lone deputy on the other side of the street. He just stood at the curb, looking at me as I approached him. I slowed my pace some, so as not to look suspicious, but he continued staring at me.

As I would with a wild animal, I averted his glare.

It was then the deputy cocked his revolver.

"And where do you think *you're* going?" he yelled, aiming his gun at me. There was a pause.

"Home!" I yelled back as I continued walking past the deputy.

Once past him, I waited until my fear subsided before I looked behind me. The deputy was no longer there.

Finding my car was like seeing a long-lost friend. But the feeling was short-lived given that John was not there. After waiting for John for about thirty minutes, I called his home from a phone booth. His father was relieved that I had called and told me that his son had checked in with him. After leaving the rally, John was able to call a relative and would soon be on his way back to Bakersfield. Despite the good news, I still felt uncomfortable. John's parents had not been keen on the idea of him going to LA with me. Before I was able to apologize though, John's father let out one of his gregarious laughs.

"You two will have something to talk about someday! That's for sure."

"That's for sure," I echoed.

At about the same time that a gun had been pointed at me by the deputy, Ruben Salazar was shot through the head with a tear gas projectile by an LA County Sheriff's deputy marksman, Thomas Wilson. Although the department claimed the death was unintentional, photos taken at the Silver Dollar bar just minutes before he was killed inside, show a number of deputies already guarding the bar's back door.

For those living on the more affluent west side of town, Los Angeles Sheriff Department's news bulletins may have seemed credible. In my mind however, knowing what Salazar stood for, combined with the evidence of the deputies being behind the Silver Dollar before the shooting, and with what I witnessed at the Chicano Moratorium rally, their credibility was shattered.

14.

Packing my suitcase at home in Bakersfield, I began thinking of how close to death I may have been that afternoon in East Los Angeles. I questioned why I'd decided not to stop when I heard the deputy tell me to. I was certain the Chicano Moratorium had changed me; I was just not sure to what extent.

After graduating from Garces High, I had decided I would go to law school after college. It was while I was in Speech and Debate at Bakersfield College, a two-year school, that I decided which law school I would seek admission to. One day, after a debate at USC, my teacher, Mary Himmelhoch, asked me what plans I had for after college. I told her I wanted to go to law school but did not know which one. Ms. Himmelhoch asked me if I had heard of Boalt Hall at U.C. Berkeley.

"No, I haven't. Is it good?" I asked her.

"It's the 'Harvard of the West,'" she assured me with a grin.

In the days following, I researched Berkeley Law, as it's now known and decided that was where I would go. Ms. Himmelhoch was happy to hear it. That decision also helped me finalize my choice on which college I would attend for my junior and senior years—San Jose State College. I had heard many stories about how politically active the student body was, in particular, the Chicano student body. Better still, it was near U.C. Berkeley.

I first discovered college catalogs while in the eighth-grade, at the library on Baker Street. For a whole year before I left Bakersfield, I spent hours studying the requirements of both schools I had settled on. Once my choices were made, these became my road maps to follow for the next seven years. As any good pilot does, I continued referring to my checklists, until I graduated with both my Bachelor and Juris Doctor degrees.

I would find, after my graduation from Berkeley in 1975, that life would never again be simple. While in school throughout my childhood, I had grappled with the reality that I didn't have a father to help me navigate during my early life. However, while reading Nietzsche's *Beyond Good and Evil,* I really connected with the idea that being a man means having a goal and knowing how to accomplish it. His writings have been inspiring to me ever since.

So, I packed everything I owned, including the *mezuzah*, into one suitcase, but I also took with me the worthy lessons I had learned at home—the dozens of Mexican "*dichos,*" or aphorisms, with which I had been instructed. Though my conscientiousness and self-assuredness would sometimes be mistaken for arrogance, my mother taught me to stand for what I believe in.

On September 12, 1970, I took the early Greyhound bus from Bakersfield to San Jose. Just a few blocks from the San Jose bus station I looked out my window and saw the Mexican Independence Day celebrations in what is now called Plaza de César Chávez.

Seeing the celebration brought to mind the *Fiestas Pátrias* in Bakersfield, and those fond memories and the colorful displays just outside my window helped me feel welcome.

The Allen Hall dormitory was to be home for the first semester of my junior year. It was one of six identical, three-story brick dorms located near the campus. Each room was configured for two roommates, which was far less space than the two rooms I had become accustomed to when Florencio had left for college. However, I found Spartan living wasn't bad for discipline.

The windows looked out onto a large, well-kept courtyard.

My main concern was what my roommate would be like. If I had to have a roommate, I preferred that he was Chicano, but for some reason, it took two weeks for the school to find anyone. On the Monday of my third week, the Resident Advisor approached me on campus and excitedly exclaimed,

"Marco, we got you a roommate!"

I pretended to look pleased. "Oh yeah? Who is it?"

"He's Chicano, from Texas, and his name's Jose Antonio Terrazas. He's already moved in."

I was told he would be returning from classes later, so I looked forward to meeting him. I went up to our room on the second floor.

I saw how clean and orderly his bed was made, and there were no clothes left strewn about. My attention was next drawn to my desk where I placed my books, and then I turned to his. His desk was also very neat. He had a large, framed picture of himself, which I thought was somewhat odd. It came across as a bit narcissistic, but I wasn't a paragon of humility myself, so I chuckled and brushed it off. I looked forward to our one-on-one meet-and-greet. I got busy with my homework, which I customarily tried to finish before dinner.

As I was wrapping up my work there was a knock at the door. It was the Resident Advisor with a thin guy who seemed nice enough, though with a nervous demeanor.

We were introduced, and the Advisor asked him to tell me a bit about himself. As he did, it dawned on me that he was not the same guy as in the large picture.

"He's gay," was all I could think of as he chatted on without me registering more than a bit of his colorful spiel. He said he was a drama student. "It figures," I thought.

I was afraid my face would betray my homophobia, which I experienced at that point in my life. I was only able to force a smile and shake his hand. I could hear Mom whisper to me, *"Guantes blancos, hijo?"* (White gloves, son?) It was a Masonic term my Mom used to say, meaning "Be respectful."

After a restless night, I awoke in a more noble spirit. I had gone to sleep thinking of how years earlier I had seriously considered going into theater arts. I studied several books, starting with the basics and including Stanislavsky's "method acting."

Strangely, I was both fascinated and repelled from pursuing an acting career. The mention of homosexuality in the theater in each of these books I read wrecked any aspirations I may have had.

Thinking of the *dicho*, "*lo cortés no quita lo valiente*," (Courtesy does not take from one's valor) I said good morning to my new roommate who was already at his desk.

I wanted to start anew with him and felt that not asking about the picture on his desk would not be neighborly of me. So, I asked him straight up, hoping only that my apprehension was not detectable.

"He's my very special friend I met at my previous college."

I was relieved I had asked and appreciated his candor. By then, he had for sure read through my country-bumpkin homophobia. His personal and political perspective was no longer relevant as he made it clear his passion was in acting and that he had no time nor interest in politics.

I expressed my welcome once again, and I set off for classes and my evening MEChA (Movimiento Estudiantil Chicano de Aztlán) meeting. I was confident that my roommate and I, though different, were capable of mutual respect.

Two weeks passed and my studying had picked up substantially. I was "in the zone" as far as academics were concerned.

Then one Saturday morning, Jose Antonio left for San Francisco. I would have the room to myself all weekend, which I thoroughly enjoyed. I was relieved by his safe return when I heard him at the door late Sunday evening. I was in the middle of a complicated passage in my political science textbook when the door opened. Without looking up I welcomed him back, but continued focusing on my work. He was chattier and more animated than usual, but I remained stoic.

I sensed him behind me giggling when I felt his light touch on my back. My scalp and the hair on the nape of my neck shivered like my *tío* Mike's horse, Colorado, when thunder would strike. I leaped up out of my chair, turned around, and sternly told him to his face,

"Look, Terrazas, I don't care what you are or where you've been. Please just don't ever lay a hand on me again. Understand?"

He nodded and his eyes teared up.

The following day, after class, I was met at the door to my dormitory by the Advisor.

"Marco, have you heard about your roommate's father?"

"No, I haven't."

"His father was involved in a very serious accident and Jose Antonio had to return to El Paso. He's cleared out of the room. It's all yours."

I had mixed feelings, and I'd like to believe I would have apologized for reacting the way I did. But that would have to wait years, as would my coming to grips with my homophobia. It was years later also that I discovered his father was never involved in an accident.

One weekend toward the end of the semester there was a loud knock at my door. It was Jess Jacques "Hawk" and Sal Arriaga, both close friends. They came in as if on official business. Hawk, a former US Army sergeant, barked out,

"We found a three-bedroom house. Want in?"

"Need to see it first," I responded, equally terse.

My next semester was a world of difference. I enjoyed the company of my new roommates, forging life-long friendships. Our new house was broken in by a party none of us, apparently, had any idea of until after a MECHA meeting.

The meeting was spirited with the election of Gabe Reyes as our new chairman. After adjournment, as people were starting out of the room, Rudy Madrid, who I hardly knew, yelled out that he had an announcement:

"FOLKS! I just want to pass on an invitation Marco has just extended. There is a party at his pad, and you're ALL INVITED..."

"WHERE?!"

Rudy had taken the liberty of writing our new address on the board. He pointed at it and concluded with,

"Be there or be square."

It turned out to be a great party, and after my first few drinks, I paid Rudy back by announcing that it was his birthday. That called for more beer, and a couple of people took up a collection. It was then I found out that Rudy had about seven birthdays throughout the year. It was his version of "public relations."

15.

During the two years I spent at San Jose State I managed to complete over 120 units, more than what was required to obtain my bachelor's degree in political science and critical to obtaining entry to an accredited law school such as Berkeley's Boalt Hall.

In my second semester at San Jose, I met Vickie Hernandez, the young woman who I would marry two years later, while in the middle of my first year at law school. Vickie and I met in February of 1971 at the birthday party of our popular MECHA chairman, Gabe Reyes. She was a senior, and I was a junior transfer student. We shared several things in common, among the most important at the time was that we were both determined to complete our respective educational goals; her goals were in journalism.

We had both been raised Catholic and had gone through a basic Catholic education, and even though neither of us practiced the faith, our principles were grounded in the Church. She had gone to school at Nativity in Menlo Park, which was mostly white and middle class, whereas I had gone to Guadalupe in a Bakersfield barrio, which was mostly Mexican-American and working class. Another similarity was that our parents were both business owners. Her father owned a cabinet shop, whereas my mother was a food product distributor.

We also marched together. That spring of 1971, after California Governor Reagan made major cuts to the Equal Opportunity Programs (EOP) throughout the state, over one hundred Mechistas from San Jose State marched to Sacramento in protest. Rudy Madrid, Ben Cadena, Adrian Vargas, Helen Najera, Sal Bravo, Lawrence Holguin, Ben Cadena, Ed Robledo, and others provided the music that motivated us and made our spirits soar through it all.

In five days, we marched approximately 120 miles. As tired as we were, Hawk, Sal, and I had a "Blister Party" at our place when we got back to San Jose. Once again, Rudy made the announcement, this time on the steps of the State Capitol. Our animal house had gone very public.

Vickie graduated a year before me and went on to the University of California at Los Angeles (UCLA) where she obtained her master's degree in journalism.

We continued our relationship by taking turns flying between San Jose and Los Angeles. The airline tickets were incredibly cheap, and either I stowed-away in Hershey Hall at UCLA, or she stayed with us in San Jose. There was never a dull moment, yet we each persevered with our studies.

As part of Vickie's thesis, she made a documentary film about a young Mexican-American man killed by the Los Angeles Police Department. It was excellent. Considering all the other factors, I felt we were a good fit.

At the end of the year, we both graduated, participating in the Chicano Commencement held at Sacred Heart Church in San José.

I was off to Berkeley.

The study requirements in college paled in comparison to those of a first-year law student, and I knew I had to buckle down. No more impromptu parties, drop-ins, or Rudy Madrid's birthdays. I missed it all at first, but as the school year wore on, I didn't have time to even reminisce. That first semester I lived in a dorm that was actually connected to Boalt Hall with its classrooms, library, and offices all accessible without having to venture out. It was like living in a Spaceship. I couldn't help but study with so few distractions. The only way to pass the time was to watch the folk dancing at the International House kitty-corner from the dorm, or our vintage pinball machines in the basement.

There was a massive amount of assigned reading covering the basics in the first year: contracts, criminal law, constitutional law, torts, and property law. There were stacks of cases to brief, analyze, and extract principles from to apply in our exams. Unlike college, which I pretty much sailed through, at Berkeley I had to study past midnight and beyond, every day. For the unquestioning mind, the study of law is a memorization exercise. But for those who question not only the law, but our societal values as well, it is far more complicated, and often even the spirit is vexed.

After my first semester, Vickie and I were married in a quaint one-hundred-year-old Catholic church near her home in Menlo Park. It was the parish church of the Catholic school she and all of her siblings had attended. Many of her extended family members came from as far away as Mexico. Fewer of my family were able to come, but it was a great time, in good company. A few of my college and law school friends were also there, including Sal Arriaga who accompanied me to the altar as my groomsman. My brother, Florencio, was the best man.

After a weekend honeymoon up the Russian River, Vickie and I settled in a small apartment in the Mission District of San Francisco, not far from Dolores Park. While she worked at KPIX, the local CBS affiliate, I finished up my first year of law school by taking the bus to Berkeley, a daily four-hour commute.

I also volunteered at La Raza Centro Legal, a service center for low-income residents of the Mission District. Under the supervision of private attorneys, we submitted our general case information from La Raza to Boalt Hall and other participating schools. The Centro had been established by, among others, brothers Al and Gary Borvice, life-long residents of the Mission District. Al and I were classmates. Years later, another student at the Centro, Frank Fernandez, from the University of San Francisco, would join me as a UFW volunteer attorney.

At the Centro I was able to see first-hand the practical applications of the courses I found difficult, shrouded as they were by legal theories. By helping the poor with their problems, the law became demystified for me. It also made law school relevant and much more interesting.

PART THREE

16.

In 1973, at the end of my first year of law school, I volunteered for Migrant Legal Services, formed by classmates Roberto Ybarra and Federico Sayre, to assist the UFW legal department. It was through the UFW legal department that I received my assignment to spend the summer as a clerk in Salinas.

I would be rooming with John Rice-Trujillo, a Hastings law student, his pregnant wife, Celia, and their rambunctious young son. My thought was that after a very busy and stressful first year in law school I could at least look forward to a tranquil summer. I would be proven wrong.

I spent the first couple of weeks in Salinas interviewing witnesses and writing affidavits. We stayed in a clean two-bedroom apartment provided by the Union. Then, it was decided by Jerry Cohen, and probably at the request of local UFW organizer Roberto Garcia, who had taken me under his wing, that I should go to Mendota and assist in the melon strike directed by Cesar's cousin, Manuel Chavez, and Roberto. Initially, I thought I would be missing out, not working under Jerry's direct supervision along with other experienced lawyers such as Bill Carder and Sandy Nathan. I had hoped I would be learning the practical aspects and fancy footwork that makes one a sharp litigator.

On the other hand, I also knew that under Roberto, Manuel, and others in the UFW, I was learning what I couldn't in school, or in any high-priced labor law firm. That was unique to living with and truly knowing the workers who were fighting for their rights to organize and for a decent living. I felt then, and still believe, that it is only by sharing and understanding the needs, passions, and aspirations of the workers that one can best advocate on their behalf.

I was at the UFW office on 14 South Wood Street in Salinas when I got Jerry's call about my assignment in Mendota. He told me to come by as there were some items he advised I should take with me. The items were: an IBM-Selectric Typewriter, a ream of white, erasable, formatted pleading paper, and a one-volume copy of the California Penal Code. Roberto had given me the heads-up earlier, and so, I had my bag ready to go. When I swung by the law office to pick up the items, Jerry said, "This is Manuel's strike, so, this should do it."

Not understanding exactly what that meant, I did not respond except to thank him. As I started out the door, he yelled out to me, "Stay in touch. And don't get arrested!"

I looked back and saw he had on a mischievous grin, difficult to read. It was then I began to suspect I was in for an adventure.

"Will do!" I said.

Roberto and I carried my "office" out the door and were gone.

Waiting outside were organizers Calacas; Gustavo Romero, aka Compis; and the enigmatic Enríque Cortéz, from Mexicali, or "*Chicali*" as the workers called it.

We loaded up and got into Calacas's car, a classic forest-green Lincoln. It wasn't a low-rider, but it seemed so because of the weight of its load. We slowly left the Salinas downtown area and got onto the 101 Freeway North.

The guys spoke about what awaited us in Mendota and exchanged Manuel Chavez war stories as I looked out the window and recalled the 1970 March on Salinas held days after the historic signing of the collective bargaining agreements by the Delano grape growers. I had come immediately up to Salinas with LeRoy Chatfield to help organize the march from King City to Salinas. It was all still fresh in my mind.

My daydreaming was interrupted from time to time by the boisterous laughter of the others, intermixed with a generous dose of music on the radio—oldies, Vicente Fernández, Ramón Ayala, and Los Tigres del Norte.

The cool breezes of the Salinas Valley were a sharp contrast to the summer heat of the Central Valley.

By the time I saw the first Mendota road sign on State Highway 33, I had already learned from Roberto about Manuel and how he ran his strikes relatively outside the general UFW mainstream. I learned he prided himself on the element of surprise, meaning taking fast, preemptive strikes. The goal to bring his target companies to their knees first, and, hopefully, obtain a quick contract. He also held a firm belief that any strikers who were arrested for strike-related activities would be bailed out and have legal representation if criminal charges were brought. This policy was based on loyalty to his strikers, but also had a practical aspect of assuring the other strikers that they too would be treated squarely.

Mendota is a city in Fresno County, California. Beginning in 1891, it thrived as a Southern Pacific Railroad storage and switching facility site. Little did the residents of the small city (population 3,000, give or take depending on the melon season) know in 1973 that their town was about to be occupied with about 200 young strikers (*huelguistas)* and five times that number of strike-breakers, "*esquiroles*," more commonly known as "scabs."

1973 was a critical year for the UFW. The contracts signed in 1970 had expired and instead of negotiating new ones with the UFW, the grape growers brought in the Teamsters Union and signed "sweetheart" contracts with them, that is, contracts in which the workers had no say. In response, the Union began a general strike in the grapes in Coachella in mid-April 1973, which by July had moved into the southern San

Joaquin Valley and beyond to Fresno County. The strike essentially followed California's seasonal grape picking, except that season we buried two strikers along the way; one dying at the hands of a scab, the other killed by a Kern County Sheriff's deputy. Deputies often acted as the growers' private goons.

The two farmworkers assassinated were Yemeni, Naji Daifallah, and longtime UFW member, Juan de la Cruz. Cesar's oldest son and my friend, Fernando, was shot at five times while acting as a California Legislative Observer on a UFW picket line. Fortunately, the five bullets hit the car, which he took cover behind. Thousands were arrested throughout the state and hundreds injured at the hands of deputies or the Teamster-bought goons imported by the growers. The Teamsters were pining for sweetheart contracts, which they got. The growers' plan was to avoid pro-worker UFW contracts at any cost.

The 200 UFW melon strikers arriving in Mendota were initially organized in the Imperial Valley. The Salinas veteran UFW organizers recruited by Manuel would be staying in an old labor camp in the heart of old Mendota about a mile from the George Pappas packing shed and a block's distance from the town's last remaining brothel.

I was assigned the small room once belonging to the camp caretaker. It was about five feet by nine feet, with old protruding cupboards. The strikers slept on the floor of the large room that once served as the eating quarters or outside in their cars. The only furnishings, other than my small cot, were a small wooden desk and chairs that I would be sharing with Roberto when he gave the strikers their weekly strike benefit checks. On it was my typewriter, paper, and the California penal code. The old black phone had not yet been connected, so until Manuel arrived, we would have to resort to using a payphone in front of *Mi Ranchito*, one of the two Mexican bars in town.

We pulled up to the parking lot to find that many strikers had already arrived and were quite anxious to meet Roberto as he was Manuel's designated organizer. A small group of them came up to the car as we got out and were happy that we had arrived. Others approached, and Roberto, in energetic fashion, began an impromptu meeting.

The first order of business was to request that all line up. We had to take down each striker's name and personal information so we could document their attendance and assure that they received their benefit payments. As this was happening, Roberto went through the basic rules of the camp. These were presented in order of importance, such as no fighting, no weapons, and no heavy drinking.

"The last leaves plenty of room for interpretation," I thought as I attempted to study their blank expressions. After the roll was taken, the strikers were each given their first check. Beginning Monday, Roberto informed them, local volunteers would be providing the day's meals, except for Sundays when they would be on their own.

Lastly, Roberto introduced me and asked that I explain what my participation was going to be as a law clerk, or "*cási abogado*," (almost lawyer). That got a good laugh.

I gave a short spiel as I saw they were now more anxious to cash their checks than listen to me. I can't say I disagreed with their priorities.

After they got their checks and said *"Gracias!"* they scattered into smaller groups. Many of them left for the small market on Main Street, returning with food, snacks, and plenty of cold beer. It was, after all, Saturday night.

In no time, I was offered a cold one, and then later, Mezcal, from a small brown bottle shaped like the agave plant. I sat near Calacas's Lincoln, listening to stories of hometowns and girlfriends in Mexico, as well as of "*la huelga al sur*," our grape strike down in southern California.

As the sun started to set, the mood picked up, as did the music which now played loudly, interspersed by Roberto's oldies tapes that he kept in a dented metal case. Someone had rigged up a small amplifier that projected all the way down to the brothel.

A couple of people broke out their guitars and Compis started the soft wailing, from oldies to Mexican ballads, with accompaniment provided by Arizona UFW member, Joe Hilyard. They played into the early morning hours.

After a few hours of sleep, Roberto banged on my door.

"Buenos días, Marco! 'Tas crudo? Vámonos a comer crawdads!" (Good morning, Marco! You hungover? Let's go eat crawdads!)

The Spanish word "*crudo*" literally means raw, but it was the secondary meaning that was much more relevant on that hot Sunday morning. The point is, I was terribly hungover.

With my head pounding, I instinctively got up and dressed, splashed water on my face, and went outside to see what the plan was. Compis was outside reading the newspaper and told me how earlier Roberto, Calacas, and he had gone out to do some scouting. They found out that the Mario Saikhon company, a key UFW target down in the Imperial Valley, would not be harvesting up in the Mendota area. So, the campaign would target, among others, Pappas and The Harris Ranch Company. Harris was huge and well-diversified, having thousands of cattle in a feedlot near Coalinga, many of them bound for Japan to be sold at exorbitant prices.

I took it all in while I scanned the dirt parking lot that had now been completely converted into a striker encampment. Most of the men were gone except for the clean-up committee that had been hastily organized Friday evening, and Joe Hilyard and his assistant, who were changing the oil of our old *Huelga* bus.

Hilyard's assistant, Paco, was short, stout, and about thirteen. His face had an uncanny likeness to that of the Mexican revolutionary, Francisco "Pancho" Villa. He was an orphan. He was also a real scrapper and perhaps it was because of this and his young age that he was adopted as the strikers' mascot. One Saturday I stopped a boxing match between Paco and a taller, larger, and older striker who clearly had the edge. Paco was both angry and embarrassed by the TKO. He pleaded with me, shaking his head, with a bruised, swollen face, red as a tomato.

"*¿Y Roberto?*" (Where's Robert?) I asked, trying to not move my head too abruptly as I spoke.

"They'll be right back. They just went to the liquor store for some beer and stuff. You going?"

I took my sunglasses out of my shirt pocket and put them on to ease the headache and hopefully stop the bluish haze that came with the *cruda* of that morning.

"Sure. I'm in," I answered, as if speaking to myself. Compis looked over at me, and said

"Hey, it's Sunday."

We weren't even twenty minutes out of the camp towards Fresno when Calacas suddenly pulled off the old, two-lane farm road. A massive dust cloud shot out behind the car as we parked right next to a Central Valley canal. It must have been 105 degrees by then. I was on my second beer and things were already looking brighter. My bluish, distorted vision began to clear behind my sunglasses. My plan for the day had been to relax, have fun, and not try to keep up with the *veteranos* (veterans of the strikes). But here I was, again. The next day we would all be on a picket line somewhere in this vast, flat hellscape, and I'd have to be up for the challenge. My middle-class, guilt-ridden mood vanished when Roberto yelled,

"*AGUAS!*" ...just as all 250 pounds of him hit the water with a thud, shooting a spray at least eight feet into the sky. *"Metanse, cabrones!"* (Get in, bastards!) he challenged us, and the party was on.

The following day I was rudely awakened by Roberto bellowing out,

"Ayer dában miedo, pero hoy dan lástima! Vámonos!" (Yesterday, you guys were scary, but today you're pitiful! Let's go!)

Roberto's energy was infectious, and there was an immediate stir about the camp, with no one questioning his authority; we all knew why we were there, and he was the man that would see us through it. We all scrambled about dressing and washing up, then went to our cars or the *Huelga* bus. Joe already had it warmed up, with Paco up front at the ready. The race in the morning was all about beating the strikebreakers to the fields to convince them to join our strike. The best time to do this was before they were driven deep into the fields in the morning. And after work, it absolutely had to be done before they were taken to the labor camps, where armed company guards would be sure to bar our entry.

Since this was our first day picketing in the Mendota-Firebaugh area, we had to see how it would go. We were all in Calacas's car waiting for Roberto, who was still barking orders at the remaining stragglers. When he returned, we rode off into the dark, early morning.

Sitting in the back, I leaned my head slightly against the window and thought about the day at the canal and the corn chips, salsa, and crawdads in their shells with fresh lemon juice. The fact that the crawdads were harvested in what was certainly a pesticide-polluted canal did not matter. We ate dozens of them and washed them down with ice-cold beer on that glorious Sunday, and we would do so again.

In 1973, Fresno County was unrivaled as the top agricultural county in the state. It encompassed almost two million acres of the richest agricultural land, and half of it was dedicated to farming over 300 different crops, some of them unique to Fresno agriculture. The industry accounted for over twenty percent of the county's jobs. It is no wonder then why the Fresno County Sheriff Department's primary task was to assure the crops moved from field to packing shed and then to refrigerated freight cars to be shipped and sold around the globe.

In that summer of 1973, it was Cesar Chavez, the UFW, and its striking members that stood to interrupt this commercial stream. And it would be the coordination between the courts and law enforcement that would be used to stop them. This would prove to be the case, despite any claims of constitutional rights of assembly or speech the Union lawyers might have asserted.

The discriminatory enforcement of the law and the lopsided court-issued injunctions, augmented the exhibition of force and threat of violence perpetrated by law enforcement on the picket lines. In this regard, I believe that whenever any worker peacefully exercising his right to assemble is forcefully arrested, violence is being inflicted upon him, or her.

The information Roberto had gathered the day before had proven to be accurate. We arrived at the exact location the *meloneros* (farmworkers who pick melons) were bussed to approximately ten minutes before they arrived. This was not an easy task, given as this corner of the world was vast and desolate compared to the rest of the county.

It was natural that the strikers bottlenecked at the entrance to the immense melon field. As the buses rolled in, the strikers, some with flags in hand, cried out to the workers about to break the strike,

"*Carnales,* únanse *con nosotros!*" (Brothers, join us!) and "*¡HUELGA!*" (STRIKE!) and "*¡Esquiroles!*" (Strikebreakers! Scabs!)

The 1973 Mendota melon strike had officially begun, and the air was charged with the strikers' energy mixed with the smell of pesticides.

The company buses revved up their engines at times to clear the way of our most exuberant members. Some workers in the busses avoided looking at the strikers. The exhaust fumes were thick and reeked of diesel. The days to come would demonstrate if this captive workforce could be called out to join the UFW as successfully as had been done throughout southern California. Manuel and Roberto were betting they would, even if it led to confrontations with those sworn to stop them.

"*¡Marco, ven! ¡Ya llego la chota¡* (Marco, come on down! The cops are here!) Time to do your thing, little brother," yelled Roberto.

Looking in Roberto's direction, I saw a long line of sheriff's patrol cars behind the last company bus, followed by two black Fresno County Sheriff busses. Most of the thirty to thirty-five deputies had on faces of stone; a few others looked to be seething with anticipation.

"*¡AGUAS!*" ("Heads up!") someone shouted from behind us.

Having been briefed by Jerry Cohen in Salinas, I knew basically what my role was, but my lack of experience added to the insecurity I momentarily felt.

Roberto snapped me out of it. He patted me hard on the back and said, "Come on Marco, let's go do some picket line protocol," as we walked toward the arriving deputies. He asked one of the first to exit his patrol car who the officer-in-charge was.

"That would be Lieutenant Hunt. He's riding shotgun, three units back."

"Is he white?" Roberto asked.

I cringed. The deputy was unable to hold back a smile. In fact, all the deputies were white.

"Yes, actually, he is. Tall, buff, looks a bit like Sergeant Rock, the comic book hero."

That comment brought a laugh out of Roberto, who had himself been a US Army veteran. I immediately surmised that humor was not only a good icebreaker but good protocol as well. So far, so good.

We met with Lieutenant Hunt and his driver outside the third car down in the line.

"Good morning gentlemen. I'm Lieutenant Hunt."

The exchange reminded me of the beginning of an NFL game before the kickoff—the shaking of hands, flip of the coin, and the calling of sides.

"Good morning officer, I'm Roberto Garcia, UFW organizer, and this is Marco Lopez, our law clerk. He'll be dealing with you and your men, as needed."

Hunt shook our hands firmly and then scanned us both from the slight distance he kept. His chiseled facial features were accented by the headlights of the patrol unit. His steely-blue eyes shone brightly. He did not come across as authoritarian, but rather, simultaneously professional and casual. He was also, unlike Sergeant Rock, impeccably dressed and well- shaven.

"Thank you for introducing yourselves. It's important for us to go over the rules of engagement at the outset. It makes things easier all around. We neither want nor expect to have things go wayward here, as they have elsewhere in the county and in southern California."

"Oh, we agree. We don't want trouble either. Have you gone over the rules of engagement with the other side?" asked Roberto.

"I have. You know their lawyers will be in court today to get an injunction against you guys for that great reception you gave their workers. The blocking of busses, shouting, and striking the windows with flags and sticks."

"Those were just little love taps, Lieutenant," Roberto offered. "If we were allowed, as human beings, to talk to the strikebreaker, there wouldn't be a need for these circuses. But we aren't, and so these little confrontations will continue. It's human nature, you know?"

Hunt paused, perhaps processing Roberto's words before responding.

"Yeah, enough for their lawyers to make a lot of money. Hey, I'm not going to tell you guys how to do your job. Just know that we too have a job to do, and like you, I'm here to make sure it gets done. Understood? Who should we serve the paperwork on tomorrow morning?"

"I'll accept service. But Marco here will act as the Union's liaison on a day-to-day basis."

"Are you a lawyer?" Hunt asked me.

"No sir, but I will be in two years."

"Then it'll be you running into court and making all the money." Both he and Roberto chuckled.

"I'm a volunteer, Lieutenant."

Hunt rested his hands on his holster and, looking out into the distance, said,

"Okay Marco, if your side has any problems or issues, come see me. Thank you, Roberto. Now let's get on with our day."

And, we did just that. Despite the excitement that started the day, the rest of the day remained relatively calm, with Roberto only commenting that the Fresno County taxpayers would be better served if deputies weren't allowed to "sit on their asses in air-conditioned cars, while everybody else has to sweat theirs off."

He asked me what my take was on Lieutenant Hunt. I mentioned he seemed even-handed enough and, at least till then, had a tight leash on his men. Roberto remained silent, chewing on a piece of grass while switching it from side to side. He turned to me and said only, "We'll see."

I took that to mean he felt the jury was still out on Lieutenant Hunt. Roberto's focus now turned to how to win the strike.

17.

The men were angry that after our third day the company buses had avoided us by leaving by a different exit. From now on we would split up into two groups to cover both exits. Roberto, while appearing outwardly cool, remained steeped in thought. It was clear he did not appreciate being played, least of all by *contratistas* (labor contractors). At the end of that day, looking as if he'd had some sort of revelation, Roberto asked me to get on the *Huelga* bus instead of in the car with him.

"Sure. Where are you headed?" I asked.

"We need to do some research. See you back at the camp. Later."

I knew that while serving in the US Army, Roberto was trained in night patrol, surveillance, and other such military tactics, and I suspected that was what he meant by "research."

As they drove off, I could hear Compis asking Roberto, "Research?" Their laughter faded off into the distance.

The bus with Hilyard at the helm was packed and ready to go. It was considerably hotter inside than outside. We were all wet with sweat, anxious for air. Some were doing *porras* and sharing humorous insights of their first day; others slept, or tried to.

"*Con ganas de apretarles los buchis a esos pinche morros esquiroles!*"

(Wish I could squeeze those damn scabs' throats!) our mascot, Paco, yelled out, provoking an uproar of laughter. It was just irreverent speech, but his delivery was great.

Then I succumbed to sleep.

Next day, I rode in Calacas' car out into the vast ocean of dark green fields. Roberto unrolled the striker sign-in list kept by Hilyard and read it out loud as we rode off to West Manning Road, a good twenty minutes away. The list was used by Manuel to confirm that strikers being paid benefits were deserving of them. Also, it helped Roberto keep tabs of who was where. Three strikers had yet to be accounted for and Roberto's concern was a rumor he had heard that they had sauntered out of "the farm" the night before and had the living daylights beaten out of them by a group of scabs.

"*Ya les he dicho a estos cabrones que no vayan al Ranchito! Es de un pinche contratista. Pa' pendejo no se estudia mano. De seguro les dieron su buena chinguiza.*" (I've told those fuckers not to go to the Ranchito! That place is owned by a fucking labor contractor. What do they expect?! For sure they got a good beating.)

After Roberto's venting none of us said anything much except Calacas, who was always relatively non-verbal,

"*Ei.*"

Roberto gave Calacas a look, then put Hilyard's list away. After a brief pause,

"Hey Compis, is Enrique okay?"

"Oh yeah, brother. I'm supposed to hook up with him later today."

Had that question not been asked, I may not have realized that Enrique did not leave with us that morning. Compared to him, Calacas was loquacious.

"He's a good *submaríno*. The best," Compis reassured Roberto.

"Oh, I know," Roberto acknowledged.

"Do you know what a *submaríno* is, Marco?" asked Roberto.

"A naval ship? No, I haven't a clue."

"A *submaríno* is basically a spy. Someone who infiltrates a company and gathers information. You know, what they call 'intelligence.' We have them, and so do the cops and companies. We all have them. It gets a little crowded and you have to be very good to not blow your cover."

"Whew. Interesting."

"They gather information about everything going on at the company, names and phone numbers of labor contractors, supervisors, company office staff, addresses, number of employees, how recruited, et cetera, et cetera. The more the merrier, like what trucking line is used, where shipments are made to. All of that shit. But most importantly, Manuel wants to make sure there's no one in the fields packing a weapon. To keep us all safe."

"Surprised Enrique would be good at it, being so quiet and all," I said.

"Oh yeah, but Enrique has two great qualities: first, *tiene oídos de tuberculoso*, he hears everything, and second, he's a real ladies' man." Roberto turned and rolled his eyes upward as if in ecstasy. We had a big laugh and then he spun around abruptly,

"*Pero quiero que sepan que Enrique respeta a las mujeres, no es como los contratistas.* (But I want you to know that Enrique respects women.) He's not like a lot of labor contractors who dog women, seducing or demanding sex in exchange for a lousy job or position. *Me vale* (I swear.)"

We arrived at the main picket site. Lt. Hunt's crew was already there, as well as a few "rent-a-cops," or private security guards hired by the Harris Ranch Company, our picket host for the day.

As soon as we parked, a deputy walked up to Roberto and handed him a brown manila envelope. Inside was a cover letter from Harris's attorney as well as a copy of the injunction obtained in the Fresno County Superior Court. TROs (temporary restraining orders) and injunctions are court orders issued, as in the growers' case, to limit the numbers and conduct of the strikers.

"*Ya vienen a joder estos güeyes,* (Here come these jerks to bother us,)" Roberto said, as he handed me the thirty-something-page-long TRO.

The paperwork would be mailed to the UFW Legal Department, located in Salinas, where Cohen would assign the matter to either one of our UFW lawyers or farm it out to a volunteer attorney. With the arrests from the grape strike climbing to 2,000, Cohen had recruited many Bay Area attorneys to assist in the defense of those arrested. But until the details of the order were hammered out in court, we would need to obey it until told otherwise by the UFW leadership.

Just east of us, in the UFW general strike in the grapes, Cesar had begun a massive civil disobedience campaign "in order to cast out the demons of injustice." He sent out the order that all arrested UFW strikers and supporters should not bail out, plead not guilty, and demand a jury trial. This held for even the most minor of offenses. In a masterful stroke, Cesar had flipped the tactic of using the legal system as a weapon against the growers, and it was choking Fresno and the other Central Valley counties with hundreds in their jails and even the fairgrounds that had to be used as a holding facility for our strikers. It was pure magic.

Based on some loose commentary we had heard, it was clear Lt. Hunt was happy to be "out west" in the melon strike instead. Little by little, we established a rapport, enough for him to confide that the Justice of the Peace out in Firebaugh told him I had the "eyes of Rasputin," whatever the hell that meant. He got a good laugh out of it.

At the end of a hot and tedious week on the picket lines, we headed back to our camp in Mendota. Although we were pleased to know that more and more strikebreakers had joined our ranks, the heat combined with the inability to reach those still working far inside the fields was wearing on the men. The other problem was that Enrique, our number one *submarino,* had reported that the main labor contractor had committed to Harris and other companies that he was actively recruiting in Mexicali for replacements to finish the season.

"He better act quickly, because it's smelling a whole lot like rotten cantaloupes out here!" Roberto commented comically to himself. It was a race against time, and Roberto set his mind to come up with a strategy.

When we arrived at camp, we heard that Manuel Chavez was in town and looking for Roberto, Compis, and Calacas.

"It's about time!" Roberto knew Manuel would embolden the men and replenish the strike fund. "We'll get *chorizo* in those burritos again, boys," he said in his native Tex-Mex drawl.

They waited outside for Manuel while I went inside to write my report. "What the hell?" I called Roberto inside. Laying on my desk, beside the California Penal Code, were three dirty security guard helmets and three empty holsters. When Roberto walked in and saw the stuff, a mischievous grin came to his face.

"Oh yeah. Forgot to tell you. Remember that rumor we heard about three of our guys getting beat up at *Mi Ranchito*? Well, we got it all wrong. It turns out they were at *Mi Ranchito* and the security guys assaulted them, but it ended up with our guys beating the shit out of *them*!" Roberto exploded in laughter.

"'*Tán cabrones!*" (What fuckers!)

I didn't laugh. Instead, I worried about the potential exposure to the Union with the evidence sitting there in front of me.

"Yeah Roberto, but why in the hell bring the crap here? On my desk!"

"*No te apures, Marco. No hay Pépe*. (Don't worry, Marco, there's no problem.) The guys were just proud, I guess."

I did not make an entry in my report.

Roberto walked back out to greet Manuel who could be heard talking in his typically emphatic and engaging way. In a few minutes, Roberto called me outside. He was standing near the *Huelga* bus, between Manuel and Paco.

"Marco, this is Manuel Chavez. Manuel, Marco is our legal beagle. He came with us from Salinas."

Manuel immediately extended his hand and greeted me warmly. His eyes twinkled intensely; his genuine interest quite apparent. He was as energetic as he was friendly and inquisitive. He peppered me with questions. I sensed he was curious as to my motives and intentions. But ultimately, it appeared I'd been adequately vetted.

"Hey, it's great to have a Chicano helping us! Do you speak Spanish?"

"*Si, claro.*" (Yes, of course.)

"*Orale.*" (Okay.)

Manuel turned his quick attention to the strikers who Roberto had assembled. They had grown now to approximately 350 men.

"*Ya me dió un reporte Roberto de su huelga. También les traigo saludos de César!*" (Roberto has already given me a report on your strike. I also bring you greetings from César!)

Manuel placed his right hand on Paco's head. "*Como se está portando Paquíto?*" (How is Paquito behaving?)

"*¡Bien!*""*¡A toda mádre!*" (Great!) The group yelled its consensus.

"*Tratenlo bien! Es de Mexicali y de hueso colorado!*" (Treat him well! He's from Mexicali and red-blooded!) Manuel responded. Paco blushed from all the attention.

Manuel continued, confiding in the strikers the details of the behind-the-scenes negotiations he was having with some of the area growers. George Pappas, Mendota's melon grower with the most seniority, had informed Manuel that he would be willing to sign if the UFW could bring the other growers to the table. He impressed upon the strikers how this was their mission.

"*Ya se los anda llevando la chingada! Gracias a Ustedes.*" (Thanks to you, they are in deep shit!) Manuel said, placing his right hand on Roberto's shoulder. "*Dénle duro y a la cabeza, y no aguantan más de dos semanas estos cabrones!*" (Keep hitting them hard and they won't take this beyond two weeks!)

"*¡La pura neta!*" (The plain truth!) Roberto added, as he raised his fist in the air.

Manuel was so effective in his ability to quickly rile up a crowd that I started to refer to him as "*El Remolino*" (The Whirlwind). The week following, on a particularly hot day, as I walked from one end of the picket line to the other, Lt. Hunt motioned to me to come over. He was standing alone near his patrol unit. Thinking that he wanted to discuss one of the terms in the injunction he appeared to hold in his hand, I did not hesitate. I crossed the two-lane country road and greeted him.

"Hey, Marco. How goes it?"

"All's well on the Western Front, Lieutenant," I kidded.

"You know, you may find this hard to believe, but I empathize with your guys."

"Oh yeah? Why's that?"

"Well, for one, I know what they're fighting for—fair wages."

"Well, yes. Better wages, along with job security and other conditions."

Hunt uncrossed his arms and we both looked out into the field at the *meloneros* working at a feverish pace.

He continued, "Marco, my parents were both dust-bowlers. They came out here from Oklahoma in the thirties and they worked in the fields, too. They worked hard, under deplorable conditions, and for miserable wages. So, they joined the Pixley strike."

The Pixley, California cotton strike of 1933 involved some 18,000 San Joaquin Valley farmworkers; black, Mexican, and white folks who fought side-by-side for better wages. After four were killed and many beaten, they were able to get a pay increase.

"Wow," was about all I could muster.

I looked over at him, attempting to better gauge his intentions, but his gaze out into the field remained fixed. There was a long pause. Hunt knew, perhaps, that he'd captured my attention. Just as I was getting ready to go back across the road, he continued.

"Yep. You know I'd like you to tell Roberto I have an idea for him to consider."

"Oh yeah? What's that, Lieutenant?"

"Tell him that if he calls off the picketing early today, saddles up and you guys go in one direction, I'll have my men do the same, and head out in the opposite direction. You guys can then come back and do what you need to do. Without hurting anyone, of course"

I was floored by what I had just heard. Initially, I thought I smelled a big rat. My facial expression must have given me away, for he was, after all, a cop with a lot of experience. He looked at me momentarily before continuing.

"Now, you know you'll only have a limited time to act. The company will be calling us, and we'll have to head right back. Do what we have to do."

Lt. Hunt looked at me, smiled, and walked away. I went the other way, to pass on the message to Roberto.

After spending six weeks with him, I was getting to know Roberto's idiosyncrasies. When he focused intently on a subject, his face would relax, to the point of letting his bottom lip drop an inch. It was far lower than an inch as I recounted what Lt. Hunt had just told me.

"What else did he say?"

"That's it, Roberto. Like I said, he made sure to add that we would only have a limited time before they would have to come back."

"*Que cabrón el güey*." (What a jerk.)

I nodded pensively as I wondered what Roberto would do.

"*Simón*." (Yes.)

"*Simón, que?*" (Yes, what?) I asked.

"*Que ya nos vamos a la chingada, dile*." (That we're getting the hell out of here, tell him.)

"*Simón, pues*." (Okay, then.)

Immediately, Roberto assigned Compis and a couple of others to spread the game plan. I went back towards Lt. Hunt and without crossing the road, simply nodded at him. He nodded back.

Within just a couple of minutes, Roberto yelled out,

"*¡Ya vámonos!*" (Let's go!) as he signaled a circular motion in the air with his index finger.

I nodded to Lt. Hunt as we passed him and he saddled up his deputies. Once we saw that Hunt had been true to his word and we were at least a mile from the scabs, we turned back at a fast clip.

The *Huelga* bus and other cars raised a lot of dust but followed close behind Calacas' Lincoln. As we sped back, Roberto made it clear to me that I should not charge the field.

"Someone will need to bail our asses out!" The others laughed.

"Oh, yeah? With what money, *carnal*?"

"You just call Manuel. He's staying at El Rancho, in Fresno."

"*Con una vieja, de seguro,*" (With a lady, for sure) Compis offered.

"*Que nuevas*!" (What else is new!) Roberto responded, to more laughter.

We had arrived back at our field. Roberto and the others quickly spilled out of the car.

I saw all our strikers, fists waving in the air, quickly preparing for the charge. Someone yelled,

"*¡HUELGA, CABRONES ESQUIROLES!*" (STRIKE, YOU FUCKING SCABS!)

Roberto, Calacas, and Compis led the charge into the field as the others followed, burning up the distance into the melon field at a furious speed. I had the urge to join them but only ventured far enough to be able to see the scabs standing up in anticipation of the fast-approaching strikers.

Paco was trying desperately to keep up, but his large hand-me-down pants, in a beautiful moment of absurdity, kept falling, and his constant tugging at the waist kept pulling him to either left or right, depending on which hand he was using to keep them up. The intention here was to scare the workers out of the field, not knock them down like the Walls of Jericho, though the decibel level must have been as the horns that brought those down.

Enrique's advance *submarino* undercover work had revealed to us that none of the foremen or workers were armed, so it was safe enough for us to rush the field.

The tactic was beginning to take effect when a large, Harris company pickup sped right toward me. It braked and it spun around in the hot dust. Somehow, I instinctively propelled my body up and backward in the air. I came down flat on my back with the left-front wheel coming to rest no more than two feet from my head. I pulled myself up as I heard the driver slam the truck door and yell,

"You son-of-a-bitch!"

I was dusting myself off when I heard Lt. Hunt, who had arrived with his men and stood behind the driver of the pick-up.

"Okay, what's going on here?"

The driver turned to Hunt, and while pointing at me, yelled, "I want this man arrested for trespassing!"

Hunt looked back to the county road and said, "Yes, you're in it, looks to me, by about ten-fifteen feet."

I shot back, "And I want him arrested for assault with a deadly weapon!"

"What weapon?" Hunt asked.

"His truck!"

"Yep. That's a weapon, Mr. Harris."

Hunt came toward me and asked me to place my hands behind my back.

"Mr. Lopez, you are under arrest, Sir. And you Mr. Harris, are under arrest for assault with a deadly weapon, i.e., your truck."

A deputy placed John Harris, son of the Harris Farms owner, under arrest and handcuffed him before placing both of us into the same patrol car. In just a few moments, we would be joined by Roberto, Calacas and Compis. We were then all read our Miranda rights by the deputy who would be transporting us to Coalinga.

The entire road became a staging area for the multiple arrests resulting from the successful charge into the field. But we were the only privileged ones making the trip to Coalinga's historic adobe jail. All the others were transported to Fresno for processing.

I was placed up front between the deputy and Harris. Awkward as that was, Roberto made it even more so as the deputy drove us out,

"*Miren a Marco—ya tiene novio.*" (Look at Marco—he has a boyfriend.) Calacas and Compis let out a big laugh. I was pissed, and given the circumstances, not very talkative.

But Roberto continued with his wisecracks,

"Marco, I want you to know, *que tú sí estás cabrón* (that you are a son-of-a-gun brother.)"

"*Porque?*" Why? I asked.

"Because you got Harris arrested for violating his daddy's own injunction. And, you got him on a felony!"

More hearty laughter came from my compatriots in the back. Even the deputy grinned, whereas Harris and I remained dead silent. The deputy sped on to Coalinga toward the setting sun.

We weren't in jail long. Within two hours, Manuel had sent a Fresno bail bondsman to bail us out of the rustic adobe jail. Harris was sprung even sooner. Most of the other *huelguistas* arrested at the field were later released in Fresno, thanks to our attorney, Bill Carder, and Manuel.

Manuel reported to Roberto that same evening that his friendly grower sources were resigned to not finish out what had already proven to be a dire season for them, but there was to be no contract signed. The smell of rotting melons permeated the melon fields when Manuel, Roberto, Calacas, and I gave Cesar a tour to show him the damage the strike had caused the growers. The Annual Firebaugh Cantaloupe Festival was canceled for the first time in its long history. In *Cesar Chavez: Autobiography of La Causa* by Jacques Levy, Cesar is quoted as saying:

"We also had great victories in 1973, in the melons and tomatoes. They're obscure because people think in terms of signed contracts, but if they think in terms of organizing people and getting their response, they're good."

And the strike had forced the growers to give all the *meloneros* a pay hike; strikers and scabs alike.

18.

In the summer of 1974, I volunteered again with Migrant Legal Services as a paralegal to the UFW's legal department. Per Manuel's request, I was assigned to Stockton to assist in the tomato strike, which extended all the way up to Yolo County and Marysville. Longtime UFW organizer, Al Rojas, whom I had met in Lamont in 1969, was in charge overall, working under Manuel Chavez.

After my finals, I drove to Stockton and was the first to arrive at the small, boarded-up building that was to serve as our office. It was a mess. It should have been boarded up before and not after it was used as a flophouse and shooting gallery. There was junk and garbage in every room of the rectangular building, which was across the street from a barrio park, surrounded by railroad tracks and a major industrial thoroughfare.

Since it was a Sunday, and I had nowhere else to go or anyone else to help me, I rolled up my sleeves, opened all the doors and windows, and began a major clean-up effort that would take hours to finish. It was dark out by the time it was clean enough to feel safe spending the night.

The next day would be Monday and I would be relieved by local volunteers and arriving staff to help with the detail work, so I crashed, serenaded by the music of neighboring lowriders who had dropped by earlier and left me a six-pack of beer and Corn Nuts.® I was grateful for their kind courtesy on this very hot June day. There must have been at least five cars guarding the UFW office that night, and thereafter. I would remain friends with them until the end of my summer in Stockton.

Early the next morning I was greeted with donuts, breakfast burritos, and hot coffee, brought to me by Rebecca, a local volunteer who stayed the entire morning to help me finish up with the clean-up. Later, Al, Manuel, and a handful of other UFW organizers from down south would arrive.

Strikes all follow a process very similar in nature, but with the added idiosyncrasies brought to it by the individual organizers. For example, Marshall Ganz was known for preparing with endless hours of meetings and detailed follow-through. His approach resembled that of a research laboratory with checklists and data-based strategy. Years later, his tactic would work for Barack Obama's first presidential campaign for which he was a chief strategist and organizer.

Al Rojas' approach, which could be just as effective, resembled the roughshod technique of herding wild horses, *"Vámonos muchachos, a pedos y a sombrerazos!"* (Let's go boys, let's get 'er done, come hell or high water!) He had no finesse, but the workers loved it. He was one of them.

Not unlike the Mendota strike, Stockton's had its interesting moments on the picket lines.

I once again communicated to the Salinas legal department any problems we encountered in the monitoring and unfair enforcement of the applicable injunctions issued by Superior Court judges.

As the strike activities mounted and one could begin smelling tomatoes rotting in the fields, the growers began to get desperate. On several occasions, a crop duster veered from its path and sprayed all of us alongside the road with a pesticide that, by law, should have been applied a good distance into the fields. We were literally wet with it. It was yet another way to attack the strikers, the other being the use of the San Joaquin County Sheriffs, who enforced the one-sided court injunctions. These two constituted the growers' air force and army: the crop-duster companies and law enforcement.

Many years later when I had left the Union and was practicing law in San Diego, I began to experience a general weakness and malaise. I consulted a specialist who took a hair specimen, which tested positive for the pesticide Malathion. The doctor asked me how I had gotten so much of it in my system. That was in 1987, thirteen years after the tomato strike of 1974. One can only imagine the health threats to workers exposed to these deadly poisons year after year, day after day.

One day, while catching up on my paperwork at the office, in walked a young Chicano kid no more than twenty-years-old, offering to volunteer. He had already approached one of our staff persons who instructed him to go to the office.

"Are you in school?" I asked.

"I'm starting college down in Los Angeles this coming Fall. But I believe in what you guys are doing and want to help."

"Well, good. Show up here tomorrow at 5:00 a.m. and you'll be assigned a picket line." I told him that if he'd like he could also apply for strike benefits and he should ask an organizer if he was interested.

"Oh, I'm okay. My dad owns a couple of bars in Los Angeles and he's covering my expenses."

"Is he paying for your car as well?" I inquired, and he simply smiled and nodded. He drove a brand-new yellow Mustang.

"Nice car," I told him.

In the following days, the young man proved to be very helpful, offering people rides to and from the picket lines, including myself and our organizers. He was handy at running errands. He never accepted reimbursement for any gas expenses, which was our ordinary practice for most volunteers.

That September, after I had returned to San Francisco and started my final year of law school, I got a call from UFW attorney Bill Carder telling me that one of our organizers had been arrested for the attempted fire-bombing of the Stockton Teamster's field office.

"Marco, no charges were filed against you because you said nothing incriminating."

"Said nothing to whom?" This was a bit nonsensical, I thought.

It turned out our new volunteer had been recording our conversations. He was working undercover for the Stockton Police Department and had wired his car. Apparently, on one of those rides when I was not in the car, the organizer had agreed to the firebombing proposed by the undercover agent.

Two weeks later Bill called me again to notify me that all charges had been dropped on a motion to dismiss. The judge agreed with Bill's argument that the defense of entrapment applied, and I would not need to testify. Bill was elated.

"Marco, one other thing. You know what some of the guys who got arrested at the Harris Ranch field were charged with?"

"I haven't a clue, Bill."

"Assault with a deadly melon. It's the joke around the courthouse." We were both still laughing when we ended our call.

When I spoke with Manuel about the undercover "volunteer," his forehead furrowed.

"*Y no me quería gustar* ése *cabrón!*" (I knew there was something off about that son-of-a-bitch.)

In the Fall of 1974, after settling into my last year of law school, Jerry Cohen called and asked me to represent the UFW in a debate to take place at the National Lawyers Guild (NLG) Convention in San Francisco. The event, he told me, would take place at Hastings College of Law, and the topic I would be speaking on was the UFW practice of calling the US Border Patrol on strike-breakers in UFW strikes. Antonio Rodriguez, a well-known and respected Los Angeles immigration attorney, was to take a position against the practice.

As I look back to 1974 and the NLG debate, I realize how vibrant the facts were in my mind. They come back to me even now with great clarity, and my position is the same now as it was then for one simple reason: In both Salinas and Stockton during my two summers volunteering, I witnessed first-hand the harmful effect scabs had on our strikes. I understood this not only from a pro-labor position, but from seeing first-hand how the strikers' morale sunk, to be lifted mainly by anger at the growers and at the scabs who at some point or other always chose to take another worker's bread and labor. I shared those feelings, and when it came time to debate our position, I did so with vigor.

When I was called to state my opening remarks on the UFW's position, the NLG members had already heard Antonio Rodriguez's address. Antonio had spoken well, and as someone who had resented the Border Patrol from my childhood in El Paso, I certainly held no brief for them. When I was five years old, whenever I saw a Border Patrol vehicle enter Dolan Place in Barrio Segundo, I would ride my bike yelling,

"*Allí viene la migra!*" (Here comes the Border Patrol!)

Antonio was applauded quite generously by those in attendance, primarily white law students, lawyers, and NLG supporters.

I first saw it necessary to set the record straight in terms of the UFW methods employed before the calling of the Border Patrol on Mexican workers. First, at the US-Mexico border, there were UFW informational pickets with leaflets in Spanish outlining what the areas and crops of engagement were. They were asked to not break the strikes, but rather, to join our striking members or work elsewhere. Second, at the arrival point, our informational picketing would take place at the labor camps where they were housed, again asking them to join us and not break our strike. They were informed of the ways the growers and contractors would exploit them as peons, while having the entire system working on the growers' side. The addresses of the UFW field offices and phone numbers were prominently displayed. I also informed the audience that the practice of calling the Border Patrol was not a common one, and in fact it was not used in either the melon or tomato strikes of 1973-1974.

An irony in this whole situation is that many of our strikers were themselves undocumented, recruited either at the border or after walking out of the fields to join our picket lines. They received the same striker stipend, assistance, and housing that all others did. There was no distinction drawn. Some stayed on, others left. Rarely did any return to break our strikes.

I spoke of the day-to-day life of the young *meloneros* (melon workers) and *lechugueros* (lettuce workers) on strike, and how I wished they could hear their stories directly, rather than from a middle-class law student. I asked them to focus on their own urban issues and to have confidence that Chicanos would sort out their own problems and issues with *la migra* (the Border Patrol.)

My talk, however, did not come off without a hitch, though not because of anything that I said. Above the applause that followed my talk, there came a loud and high-pitched yell from someone standing at the back and center of the hall,

"CESAR IS NOTHING BUT A FUCKING MACHO!"

The protestor got a mixed response; some booing, some applause, and even some hissing from those now standing. Instead of responding to him, I walked over and shook hands with Antonio, who was quite pleasant.

"Suerte, Carnal." (Good luck, Brother.)

There was one final hurdle for me, however, and that was passing the state legal bar examination at the end of my third year. Truthfully, I struggled with it. I resented being tested just after undergoing final examinations and completing research papers for my classes.

Further distracting me were the used bookstores along the way to my classes in downtown San Francisco, where I would spend hours reading about everything but the law. I figured that after denying myself outside reading for three years, I owed it to myself. Being as I was, unprepared and resentful, I failed the examination the first time I took it.

Jerry Cohen then decided that I should work for the Agricultural Labor Relations Board (ALRB), the board which had been established to administer the farmworker labor law (ALRA) passed in 1975.

Although my first choice was to work in the UFW legal department, I accepted, and LeRoy Chatfield picked me up as his law clerk. LeRoy had been appointed by Governor Jerry Brown as one of the five original board members, and it was great working with him, having known him at Garces and working together in the UFW the summer before heading to college. Vickie was hired to schedule the ALRB-conducted elections under the supervision of the Board's executive secretary, Annie Gutierrez.

Unfortunately, before the end of 1975, the ALRB was derailed when the funding ran out and the rural legislators, both Republicans and Democrats, refused to refund it.

Being without a job now, I convinced myself that to pass the bar exam, I would need to live a spartan life, alone. So, after living in Sacramento for almost a year, Vickie and I separated. She returned to live in San Francisco where she went to work at KQED with her friend, Belva Davis, and I remained in Sacramento to study for my second attempt at the bar exam.

However, before beginning my two-month study for the bar exam, I went to Yolo to visit my friends. Through the years, the Arriaga family had become like my own, and I would visit them frequently. On this occasion, I announced that I would be a recluse while I studied, as there was no way in hell that I would take the exam a third time. To make sure I'd pass, I also decided that during those two months I would abstain from alcohol.

It was a warm spring day, and as the word of my study plan got around the hamlet of Yolo, the Arriaga ranch soon became the site of a "farewell party" for me. The party went well into the night. The following morning, Sal Arriaga, his older brother Kickers, and I were *crudos*. So, we went to Jody's Place in Woodland to have a healing bowl of *menudo*.

When taking our order for three *menudos*, the waitress asked us what we'd each like to drink.

"El que no se cura, se aguzana" Kickers responded authoritatively. And who could argue with that.

"Okay, three beers it is," she said as we handed her our menus.

During breakfast and the ice-cold "hair of the dog that bit us," we discussed the serious drought in the area and how it was affecting the people of Yolo. I had already noticed there were water hoses crisscrossing backyards, used for sharing water with neighbors whose water pumps did not go deep enough to compete for water. Due to the drought, the water table was lower than it had ever been. The growers' wells were very deep so they were unaffected. Instinctively I offered, "Let's organize a water march to Sacramento to get some help."

Perhaps on this particular morning when I was hungover and craving water, the issue of water seemed especially critical.

I reiterated, "Yes, a march, and in the next month while we organize it, we'll have to develop a more detailed plan as to what we'll ask Assemblyman Vic Fazio for when we get there."

"Sounds like a good plan," Sal agreed.

We all agreed and toasted to it with another ice-cold round. The plan was on.

The march was organized by way of regular meetings and the formation of committees. The first was the organizing committee. Our mutual friends Joe Moreno, Francisco "Kickers" Arriaga, and Isabel Chavela Hernandez were among the active members.

The whole of the town of Yolo came together. Women, the elderly, children, and men marched for three days to the state Capitol. They camped out at night and had their dinner prepared by the food committee, with music provided in the country surroundings by the entertainment committee.

As a result of their efforts, the people of Yolo were able to obtain state funding for a community well. But, most importantly, for the first time in the former county seat's history, the people established their own water district that continues to thrive to this day.

19.

In late 1976, Dolores Huerta recruited me to work as an attorney for the Martin Luther King Jr. Farmworkers' Fund (MLK). At the time, I had a teaching position in sociology at Sacramento City College, thanks to my friend Chavela Hernandez. I developed and taught a course I called "Major Minorities in the U.S." I was enjoying it greatly, but since I had passed the bar exam, I decided that after the end of the fall semester it was time to return to the UFW.

The MLK Fund was funded in part by the contributions of growers who were under contract with the UFW, but by law was a separate non-profit from the UFW itself. Funds were used to provide service centers for farmworkers throughout California. Kickers and I drove from Yolo to the MLK board meeting in Calexico in my vintage Volvo. The heater was out, and it was cold.

At the meeting in Calexico, the MLK director, Ann McGregor, introduced me to the Board and asked that I tell them something about myself. I kept it brief, basically highlighting the UFW people I had worked with through the years. After the meeting adjourned, I was given the MLK Service Center attorney position and was assigned to work in Delano starting January, 1977. Cesar was the first to comment.

"Thank you, Marco. It's good to have you onboard."

"Thank you."

It had been nine years since I'd first encountered him at the gasoline coop in Forty Acres in Delano as a high school senior. I was now twenty-eight.

Kickers and I gave Dolores a ride to Stockton, over the Grapevine and up Highway 99. Although the top of the Grapevine was blanketed by snow, Cazadores® and Dolores's fascinating stories kept us warm through the long night.

As with Cesar, I had a lot of respect for Dolores, and after spending hours on this drive I got to know her better. She and I became fast and loyal friends and remain so to this day. Cesar and I, on the other hand, did not get close until much later.

Because of two speeding tickets I had on my record from before I joined MLK and because MLK was self-insured, I was forbidden by Cesar from driving my first six months. The silver lining was that I had to live at the Paulo Agbayani Village, a retirement home where many of the Filipino strikers of 1965 lived, or the "Brothers," as we referred to them. Because the Delano Field Office and MLK Service Center were located on the same property, I could walk to work.

Agbayani Village is a beautiful, mission-style adobe structure built by many volunteers. It is located on the farmworker movement property known as Forty Acres, located just west of Delano on Garces Highway, across the street from the Voice of America radio towers. What made it an oasis were the myriad of plants, trees, palms, and flowers. All the Brothers took great pride in planting and caring for them.

Talk about an education. The Brothers not only taught me about their struggles in coming to this country and their early unionizing efforts, but also about their country's long struggle for liberation, beginning with the Spanish, and their liberators, such as José Rizal. They also taught me about fighting roosters.

The fighting cocks were kept in cages outside my bedroom window. Very early every Sunday morning, I would hear the Brothers' voices and the birds' cooing intermingle. They were beginning their long day, with as much potential for triumph as there was for failure. I quickly learned that the Filipino and Mexican cultures, history, and perspectives are quite similar.

I had it made. I ate all three meals communally with the Brothers. The dishes were rich and tasty, steamed rice was the mainstay, and fresh coffee was never lacking, thanks to Tonya and Ramón who managed the Village. My commute was an easy three-minute walk across the alkaline-laden property. On a full moon, the ground was luminous.

That winter in Delano was particularly cold and foggy. I recall one day betting with my coworkers, Tony Bañuelos and Cynthia Bell, that I would go outside and not be able to see my hands extended out in front of me. Well, I'll be damned if it wasn't true.

I interviewed people with all kinds of legal issues: work-related injuries, landlord-tenant, family issues, immigration, small claims, contracts, consumer fraud, and so forth. Many of these cases were handled by Tony and Cynthia who had years of experience at the service center. Some we referred out to attorneys in the area, while others I handled myself.

One case involved Oscar, a freshman at Delano High School. While involved in a fight with another student, he "accidentally" struck a teacher with a belt while using it to ward off his attacker. That was his story, and after viewing the scene, interviewing classmates and witnesses, the youth and his witnesses, including his girlfriend, I believed there was a viable defense.

I looked forward to the juvenile court hearing with some anxiety but was fairly confident it could go well for Oscar. We all traveled together in one car to the Juvenile Court in Bakersfield — Oscar, his girlfriend, his two witnesses, and me. Cesar had lifted my driving suspension by then, so I drove.

I was vaguely familiar with Judge Jelletich, who would preside over the hearing. Years earlier, he had been my mother's judge in her divorce from my stepfather. I recalled him being courteous and friendly to all in his courtroom, especially to her lawyer, Frank Wooldridge, given as they had known each other many years. I did not expect him to remember me, but any information about a judge can prove valuable or as in this case, at least make one more comfortable. It is somewhat akin to knowing the enemy.

Once the case was called it went rather quickly, even with the Judge himself asking a number of questions. I hoped that might be a good sign, but it wasn't.

Then it was over. Because of the nature of a juvenile custody proceeding, there was no actual finding of guilt, but Judge Jelletich did "sustain the petition," which had the same effect. Also, due to that nature there was no actual sentencing, but Oscar was detained in juvenile hall until his next hearing, a month away.

The next case was quickly called, and we were soon back on the 99 headed to Delano. It was a short ride under most circumstances, but the mood in my car was somber and quiet. At least fifteen minutes passed with no one saying a word. Then Jimmy, the one witness whose testimony had in my mind been somewhat doubtful, broke the silence.

"Mr. Lopez, can I ask you a question?" he inquired.

"Of course, Jimmy. What is it?"

"Have you ever lost a case?"

"No."

"Wow."

The fact of the matter was that Oscar's case was my first trial.

That night I licked my wounds at Peoples' Bar in Delano by playing pool and listening to oldies music with Alberto Escalante, *El Malcriado's* up-in-your-face cartoonist and UFW organizer. He had recently arrived from the strike in the Imperial Valley and was also living in Agbayani.

People's was a UFW-friendly bar, and at times one could drink in the company of UFW veterans. When Dolores and Richard were there, along with Ben Maddock and other veterans, it would get downright festive, *pachanga segura* (a sure party).

20.

The following morning, while having a coffee and filing away Oscar's court documents, Cynthia knocked on my door,

"Marco, there's a call for you from La Paz."

"Is it Ann?" I asked.

She now opened my office door and with a mischievous smile said, "No. It's Cesar."

She knew I was a little out of sorts and seemed to enjoy increasing my stress level. I had never gotten a call from Cesar before that day. Little did I know he was about to give me my first assignment.

"Do you want me to take a message?" she teased.

I gave her a look, then lifted the phone.

"Hello, Cesar?"

"Hi, Marco. I'm in a board meeting right now, but listen, we just got word that there's been a drowning in El Paso of a young farmworker. Esther, what's his name? Oh yeah, Ramón Longoria. The information we have is that he was drowning in the Río Grande and that rather than help him, the Border Patrol dunked him with a pole of some sort."

"When did this happen?"

"Yesterday, so we need you to fly to El Paso and investigate immediately."

"When would you like me to do that?"

"Today."

"Today?"

"Yes. I'll put Ann on, and she'll schedule your flight and make other arrangements. Come see me when you get back."

"Of course. Who should I contact there in El Paso?"

"Go to the Mexican General Consul in El Paso. Introduce yourself and tell him why I've sent you."

"Very well then, I'll report to you as soon as I get back."

"Good deal."

In a few hours I was at LAX boarding a direct flight to El Paso, Texas. Ann McGregor, MLK Director, had booked an open flight and made available a three-day per diem, which was more than adequate, given my assignment. During my flight, many childhood memories flooded my mind about when my mother, after her divorce in Douglas, Arizona, took my brother and I to live there. She worked as a civil servant with the U.S. Army in Fort Bliss, packing parachutes, mending Fort Bliss and White Sands officers' uniforms, and other things. I was three and my brother was six.

Perhaps it was because I absorbed my mother's melancholy during the five years that we lived there that I didn't particularly like El Paso. But it was the area's severe weather contrasts that I blamed, instead of my melancholy.

I turned to my few notes in the case and wondered what evidence and witnesses I might be able to discover in Ramon's drowning-death. I thought, too, of how many times I had crossed into Juarez with my mother and Florencio, always close at her side, as she tightly held our hands.

Out of my window I spotted the Franklin Mountains.

It was an overcast, cold day when I exited the terminal and found a Yellow cab. As it turned out, Ann McGregor had me staying in a hotel conveniently located just a couple of blocks from the Mexican Consulate.

Once in my room I called and reached the Vice-Consul of

"*Protección*." This division of the Mexican Consulate's office deals with the myriad of issues confronting the Mexican citizen in any host country. This would include the drowning of Ramón, whether accidental or intentional. Since Spanish is my first language, I was well equipped to handle the obstacles and pretexts the Vice-Consul put in front of me when I requested to meet with the *Consúl General*, as Cesar had instructed me. After five minutes of her song-and-dance routine, I had my appointment.

"I reiterate counselor, only for ten minutes."

"Yes, yes. Only ten minutes. Thank you, ma'am." Since I was only granted ten minutes with the Consul, I wasn't expecting much from him.

I quickly showered, put on a fresh shirt and tie, and rushed out. I had plenty of time, but I would rather be a few minutes early, than late.

Maricela was the *Vice Cónsul de Protección* who would be introducing me to *Consul General,* Acuña-Romero. She was pleasant and reserved, and I speculated she may have spent years in Catholic schools. She was pleased, however, that I was early, for she quickly ushered me to his office, offering only that he could see me early.

When at the end of our earlier phone conversation the Vice-Consul had made sure to tell me that I would only have ten minutes with Acuña-Romero, I don't believe she ever thought I would hold to my promise. But immediately upon shaking the General Consul's limp hand, I knew that I would not be getting any useful information here.

I did as Cesar instructed me. I explained in as much detail as I could why Cesar had sent me. Both of their faces were blank.

To begin with, the two claimed not to know of any drowning of any Mexican citizen in the Río Grande. It could have been true, but doubtful.

"Maricela, do you know anything about this?"

"No, Mr. Consul."

Immediately, out came the same limp hand, and my protocol visit was over.

"*Muchísimas gracias,*" I said, as I shook his hand firmly in response.

The same with the Vice-Consul.

I told myself, "I, too, can be laconic," and did not wait to be escorted out of the office.

On my walk back to the Hotel Paso del Norte, I pondered what might have gone wrong with the meeting, and why, despite my questions, they both had expressed not even a hint of cooperation or interest in the death. Was it because of the information we had that it might have involved the Border Patrol? Could it have been because Ramón was a farmworker? They seemed not to have even known who Cesar was. He had been on the cover of *Time Magazine*, so that was hard to imagine.

I was stumped. It was as if Texas was another universe. I mused and chuckled.

Because the weather had turned for the worse and it was already dark, I decided I would have an early dinner, hop into bed, read my book, and start my day before sunrise.

"Good deal." Cesar's words echoed in my mind.

The next morning, I was up and had already showered when I got my wake-up call. I grabbed my micro-cassette recorder and went downstairs to have the continental breakfast that came with the room and included a free copy of the *El Paso Times*.

As I ate and drank my coffee, I scanned the paper for any articles relating to Ramon's drowning. No luck. There was an article on how the weather tower of the El Paso Gas building downtown had been refurbished. Now that jogged some memories. The tall, oblong, glass structure that sat atop the vintage building announced the weather, based on the color it was on any particular day.

Whatever the weather was going to be on this day, I had to get out the door and to the Río Grande river, which marked the border between El Paso and Juarez. It was a short walk to the border, but then I would be walking all day long if necessary.

Momentarily, I was walking down El Paso Street. I thought it pleasant to hear people wishing "good morning," and "*buenos días.*" I missed those courtesies not frequently encountered in other areas. It was the bi-cultural, bi-lingual, friendly way that I had been exposed to from birth. But this civility all but disappeared the closer I got to the Río Grande.

I immediately sensed a certain pall, or somberness, descend on what may well have been the poorest section of El Paso, "*El Chuco*." Dilapidated houses, many of them covered in graffiti, wound their way down, serpent-like, to the river. It wasn't the poverty that caused my uneasiness, however, but the abundance of occult and satanic symbols I saw everywhere. I also sensed unease in the faces of some of the residents, including the many young people dressed in black. The stares I was getting didn't help.

At any rate, my investigation here turned out as unproductive as my visit to the Mexican Consulate office. Every person I asked for information at the river gave me the same zombie-like response; a slight shaking of the head with a blank stare. There was a reluctance, or maybe a fear of engaging me in conversation. In a flash of insight, I thought it best to conduct my investigation from the other side of the river, known in Mexico as the *Río Bravo*.

I did not hesitate. I came back around to El Paso Street and headed south to *Puente Libre*, the oldest bridge connecting the sister cities of El Paso and Juarez. My instincts told me the investigation would go better in Mexico.

In 1989, when practicing law in Los Angeles, I stepped into the trial of Richard Ramirez, "The Night Stalker," to see how it was going. I made eye contact with him during a brief, morning break. I could also see that he had groupies in the audience, giggling with him. They were all dressed in black. At that time, I thought back to my experience in 1977, when in search of clues to Ramon's death, I walked Ramirez's El Paso neighborhood by the Río Grande. Richard Ramirez was but seventeen-years-old then; the waste was very sad.

As I walked over the bridge toward Juarez, the sun shone for the first time, producing a multitude of colorful rays with each ripple in the *Río Bravo*.

After a brisk walk, I entered Mexico at the peak of its mid-morning bustle. The noisy traffic was already reaching a crescendo. The mixed scents of food, taverns, and exhaust fumes were prevalent here on Juarez's main street. I stopped at a newsstand and got *El Diario*, one of Juarez's major daily newspapers. I read it while drinking a *café de* ólla and eating a freshly-made *churro* at a nearby stand.

Again here, as in the *El Paso Times*, there was absolutely nothing concerning any drowning at the border. I asked the news vendor, and although he didn't know anything about it, he did appear interested, if not puzzled. He pointed out how I could best reach the *Río Bravo* from the downtown area I was in. I figured that on the way to the river's edge, I would ask any Juarez policeman I might come across for information.

As on the El Paso side, the closer I walked toward the river, the denser the vibrations were. Except that in Juarez, they emanated mostly from the *Zona Roja*, the "Red Zone," where thrill-seeking tourists, many young servicemen from Fort Bliss and beyond, spent the night in the cheap bars, drinking and tipping the dance girls, who for a negotiable fee could be taken back to some room that smelled like rancid beer and *Pino-Sol*.

As I passed these "dens of iniquity," as one Apostolic hand-out called them, the *Pino-Sol* was flowing freely onto the freshly-swept, though badly-cracked sidewalks. Here, people were very much alive, with intense dispositions, all eager to meet the day.

Beer delivery trucks jockeyed for position as traffic cops moved in for their kill; *las infracciónes, multas, o mordidas* (citations, fines, and/ or bribes). I targeted one of the cops who was standing on the sidewalk for questioning.

"*Buenos días, oficial.*" (Good morning, officer.)

"*Buenos días joven. En qué podemos ayudarle?*" (Good morning, young man. What can we help you with?)

"*Ando investigando la muerte de un joven que se ahogó en el río hace unos tres días. Por casualidad no sabe algo usted al respesto?*" (I am investigating the drowning death of a young man at the river, some three days ago. By any chance do you know about this?)

"*No, fíjese. De eso no sé nada. Pero anoche, aquí se ahogaron muchísimos! Ya se los llevó la perrera a unos.*" (No, I know nothing about that. But last night, many drank themselves to oblivion here! They have already been taken to jail in our van.)

It took me a moment to pick up on his humor. Then the officer left abruptly to go issue his next driver citation and to collect his next *mordida pa'l cafecíto.*

I negotiated the remaining busy streets of *La Zona* and finally reached the riverbank, where immediately I was surrounded by six young boys, aged between five and seven. The lead boy approached me.

"*Señor, le podemos ayudar*?" (Sir, may we help you?)

He scanned me from head to toe. I did the same and noticed his shoes were both worn out at the front, exposing his toes. He gave me a big smile and continued, now sounding more like a tour guide.

"*Busca algo en particular? O solo viene a conocer nuestro famoso Río Bravo*?" (Are you looking for something in particular? Or have you only come to discover our famous *Río Bravo*?)

His whole entourage laughed. They were eager to be of help, and so I opened up to them.

"*No. Yo ando investigando la muerte de un tal, Ramón Longoria, un joven campesino que fue ahogado en el río. Acaso ustedes saben algo*?" (No. I am investigating the death of one Ramón Longoria, a farmworker who drowned in the river. Do you by chance know something?)

The young spokesman immediately took on a more serious expression and turned to his friends for some kind of reaction. They in turn also became more serious, like they might have known something but didn't feel safe telling a stranger.

"*Y si le ayudamos...nos compra algo de comer?*" (And if we help you...will you buy us something to eat?)

Before I could answer, there was one further request from another of the boys,

"Más sodas?" (Plus, sodas?)

I looked at each of them and accepted their offer, knowing in the back of my mind that if they helped me crack the case, they would each get more than simply meals and *sodas*. We all shook hands and the quest was on.

Once our deal was struck, Beto, the group's spokesman, became my "lead man." He was a natural, so much so that I asked him whether he had ever investigated before. He gave me a strained and somewhat comical look, so I thought it best not to press him.

Beto immediately called out orders to the others to fan out and ask anyone they encountered about Ramón Longoria, his drowning, and where he lived. His pack did just as he asked them to. From time to time, Beto would whistle out to any of them, or all of them. It was a very effective way to communicate one's whereabouts as well as status, all in a language known only to them. After one such exchange, I heard,

"*Neto anda perdido.*" (Neto's lost.) Beto spoke under his breath. Beto was concerned for Ernesto ("Neto") who might have gotten lost or sidetracked somewhere.

As the day wore on, I became aware of the presence of suspicious people who now also roamed the area. Then I heard a whistle.

"*Allá anda el cabroncito. Todo bien.*" (He's over there, that li'l son-of-a-bitch. All's well.) Neto, who was the youngest of Beto's group, had checked in with his trademark whistle, and Beto looked as relieved as I was.

For hours, broken up only by our lunch at a lively *lonchería* and a couple of short soda breaks, we all scanned the area repeatedly until the sun set. Soon it would be dark, and we were yet to find a single clue. I thought we should call it a day, but the boys insisted we continue, so we walked slowly back in the direction of the *Zona Roja*, and the bridge that I would take back to the comforts of El Paso.

I looked down and saw how my Johnston & Murphy capped-toe shoes were muddied and damp. Smiling, I thought, what a better choice it had been to see the Mexican Consul before the search, rather than after. My shoes would not have made a great impression either.

At this point I was rooting for the boys, who continued energetically scouring the shores of their river. They were river urchins, for lack of a better term. They all lived in a hovel, an abandoned structure, by the edge of the river. They had each other's back and lived communally.

It was nearing nine o'clock when two of the boys raced toward us from a good distance, yelling,

"*¡No fué Ramón, el que se ahogó! ¡Fué Ramona!*" (It wasn't Ramón who drowned! It was Ramona!)

My mind went blank, hearing that it might have been a Ramona, and not Ramón, who drowned at the border. Even without hearing more, it didn't make sense, and what's more, I wasn't convinced. How could we have gotten it so wrong? I was confused, tired, but re-energized, now that we had a lead.

After the two boys caught their breath, I began to question them. Beto stood next to me.

"*Con quién hablaron? Quien fué que les dijo de Ramona*?" (Who did you speak to? Who was it that told you about Ramona?)

"*Fué el Señor Rojas, dueño de la tiendita El Porvenir! El sabe todo*." (It was Mr. Rojas, owner of the store El Porvenir! He knows everything.)

"*Y dónde está el?*" (And where is he?)

"*En su tienda. Pero nos dijo que el no quiere problemas, que habláramos mejor con una viejita, una tal—Nana*." (At his store. But he told us he doesn't want any problems, that we should instead speak with an elderly woman, Nana.)

"*Y les dijo donde vive ella*?" (And did he tell you where she lives?)

"*¡Si! Nosotros lo llevamos, Licenciado.*" (Yes, we'll take you, Counselor.)

It seemed we finally had a solid lead.

"*Pues, vamos!*" (Well, let's go!)

Beto and I followed our guides to the woman who possibly knew about who we were looking for. I knew I would soon have to part from my new friends of the *Río Bravo*, and it saddened me. We had all shared quite an experience and one long day together. I would miss them.

Upon arriving at Nana's, I gave each of the boys ten dollars. They were exuberant, reaching out to shake my hand and some even hugging me.

Then, they waved goodbye to me and left as I began to climb an old wooden stairway.

Nana's dilapidated shack was perched atop what looked to be an abandoned building. I was careful climbing the shaky stairs and happy to see a dim light on inside when I finally reached the door. I knocked and waited.

The door opened, and an elderly woman asked me what I needed, peering at me with a guarded position. I told her my name and that I had been sent by Cesar Chavez to investigate a death by drowning of Ramón Longoria, a farmworker. I added that we had learned where to find her from Señor Rojas. It was then that she asked me to come in.

"*Pásele joven, a lo barrido. Yo soy, Nana. A sus órdenes.*" (Come in young man. I'm Nana, at your service.)

Inside the sparsely furnished home was a lit kerosene lamp that cast a warm, subdued light. Nana invited me to sit at the small table on which the lamp sat. Having been on my feet for most of the day, I gladly took her up on her offer.

"*¿Nos tomamos un Cafecito?* Véngase." (Shall we drink a little coffee? Come on over here.)

"*Perdone la molestia señora.*" (I am sorry for the intrusion.)

"*Nada de eso. Había yo presentido. Ya vera, aquí nos vamos a confesar.*" (No bother. I had a premonition. You'll see, we're going to "open up.")

While the coffee boiled, I hesitantly asked Nana if it was okay that I record our conversation to give Cesar an accurate report. She readily agreed, adding, "*Aquí no hay secretos.*" (Here there are no secrets.)

Nana's coffee, I found, was as strong as her character. While we drank from her pastoral *tasas de peltre*, enamel cups, I was reminded of my visits to *La Norteña*. I turned on my micro-cassette recorder and she asked a question,

"*Que sabe usted, de Ramona?*" (What do you know about Ramona?)

"*Aparentemente nada.*" (Apparently, nothing,) I answered.

From the beginning of our visit, over cups of coffee, Nana gave me more information about Ramona than I could have ever known to ask about. She explained how as a young boy he had become orphaned and, as many children do, had come to live at the *Río Bravo*. She estimated he was five or six at the time. Two years later, she heard rumors that a boy was being sexually assaulted by some of the older boys. It upset her to hear this and she went down to the river to investigate. There she would meet Ramón, who was called Ramona by the boys.

"*No se. Su mentesita como que ya había cambiado, Señor Licenciado. Ella ya se creía muchachita, y nada que yo le dijera la convencía que no.*" (I do not know, Counselor. By then she believed herself to be a little girl, and nothing I said convinced her otherwise.)

Nana stated this with a far-away expression, as if struggling, even then, to understand.

"*¿Que le paréce?*" (What do you think?)

I took it as a rhetorical question, nodded my head in understanding, and remained silent.

"*La llevé a ver al Padre Solís, el sacerdote, de aquí abajo, y me dijo que en su opinión, Ramona estaba poseída y necesitaba un exorcismo.*" (I took her to see Father Solís, the priest, from right down here, and he told me that in his opinión Ramona was possessed and needed an exorcism.) "*¿Que ridículo, no?*" (How ridiculous, right?)

I nodded instinctively and sat there numb, thinking this was way out of my league. I momentarily flashed on Beto and his friends who had helped me get to Nana's. The strong coffee and unusual story I was hearing, made me feel light-headed. Nana could sense it, could see through me, and so, she changed her pace.

"*Licenciado, Ramona no era campesina. Ella limpiaba casas, en El Paso. Mi linda muchachita,*" she said, looking over her shoulder. (*Licenciado,* Ramona was not a farmworker. She cleaned homes in El Paso. My beautiful girl.)

Nana was now visibly sad. And frankly, so was I.

Some moments passed and all that could be heard were the howling winds that had picked up steadily during our long talk, causing the flimsy house to shiver with each gust. Nana, now composed but with tearful eyes turned to me and asked,

"*¿Quiere ver su cuarto?*" (Do you want to see her room?)

The question stunned me as in a strange way I felt we were in her presence.

"*¿De Ramona*?" (Ramona's?)

From when I was first let into Nana's home, I had noticed a section in the corner set apart by colorful curtains. From time to time, I had noticed flickers from small votive candles glowing from behind them.

"*Si Nana, claro.*" (Yes Nana, of course.)

Nana and I both rose and she walked me to the curtains that served as the doorway. She opened them for me so that I could look inside. Out of respect as well as some trepidation, I did so while remaining at the entrance.

"*Pásele Licenciado López, por favor.*" (Please come on in, Counselor Lopez.)

Nana made way for me to enter Ramona's room.

Inside, three blood-red votive candles flickered and reflected warmly against a faded wooden statue of *Jesús*. Unpredictably, with the dancing light, the small statue appeared to sway—steady, then shifting in its place, swaying its face, robe, hips, and torso with every pulsating flicker.

Nana pointed out that this was Ramona's altar, at which she prayed. Since her visit to the church, when the priest suggested she should be exorcised, Ramona never again set foot there.

"*Era muy buena muchacha, Ramona. Ella nunca quiso andar suelta en las calles. Años pasados, si la invitaban a ir a fiestas y hasta cantinas. Pero ya después ni eso—porque no salía. Del trabajo se venía directamente a casa. Su humilde casa, Licenciado.*" (Ramona was a very good girl. She never was one to run loose in the streets. In years past, she would be invited to go to parties and even bars. But after time passed, not even that, because she did not go out from work, she would come straight home. Your humble home, Counselor.)

"*Gracias, Nana.*"

Nana asked that I look at her dresses, all neatly arranged in a makeshift closet. She pointed out again that Ramona was a good girl, and that rather than go out, she preferred her two passions: her dresses and cosmetics, that she wore for work; and cleaning houses in El Paso.

Nana had referred her to a family she used to clean for, the Silvers. A "nice, professional family," as she put it. Nana held back tears as she told me that they were very sad to have heard about her death and had already contributed toward her funeral expenses.

Nana confided in me that she felt confident she had helped shape Ramona's life admirably well. Oh sure, it had been difficult for both of them at times, at other times going far beyond Nana's comprehension, but she had never wavered from the task she had so willingly assumed. She had never judged and had always remained more loving than spiteful. God only knew, how at times it had been her pure anger and cunning that had protected them both from the ever-present snares of "*La Zona Roja*" (Red-light district). But in the end, it was Nana's love for Ramona that had won the day. That much was certain.

Ramona had been heaven-sent, and Nana was grateful. It was Ramona who had in recent years taken on more and more of the burden. It was she who recently had taken charge, working hard in El Paso, running the errands, and providing for them both. To Nana, it was also Ramona, the young "crowning beauty," who added joy to their humble household. They both had felt blessed as family.

She now prepared for Ramona's funeral and burial, with a strong faith that she would make it through it all. Nana saw me to the door, hugged me goodbye, and blessed me.

"*Dios lo bendiga, Licenciado.*" (God bless you, Counselor.) Nana's blessing meant more to me than she could have known.

Back at La Paz, Esther kindly asked that I wait a few minutes for Cesar to arrive from the North Unit, where he had been meeting all morning. I helped myself to some coffee and took a chair right above the basement office, which I would occupy in six months as Cesar's new in-house counsel. As I waited, I took my notes and the micro-cassette recorder from my briefcase.

NOTES TO CESAR:

Re: R. Longoria (1) Upon arrival, met with Mexican General Consul...generally uncooperative and mum; (2) Search on U.S. side proved unproductive; (3) Search on Mexican side along Río Bravo, with assistance of river friends, was successful; (4) *Ramón/Ramona* dichotomy; "Ramon" lived her adult life as "Ramona" (for details I am providing you with a tape-recorded interview of one "Nana," surrogate mother); and Ramona did not do farm work, she was a housekeeper in El Paso; (5) It appears that Ramona drowned when she fell into the *Rio Grande* accidentally; she could not swim...no evidence found that she was dunked by Border Patrol, with whom she apparently had maintained a generally good rapport; and, (6) Ramona was, according to Nana, orphaned in southern Mexico at a young age, with no known surviving family members to bring a wrongful death lawsuit.]

After our meeting, I gave Cesar my report as well as the micro-cassette interview with Nana and returned to Delano. Because of the press of Union business at hand, Cesar and I never again spoke about the Ramón/Ramona case.

21.

The Union's La Paz headquarters had been a former Kern County tuberculosis sanitorium, situated at the small town of Keene. Blue oak woodlands mixed with areas of foothill pine and grasslands are the predominant vegetation. During the dry season the grasslands take on a golden color, but in the rainy season they turn a rich green that is highlighted by splashes of color painted by a broad palette of wildflowers. On a hike up to Three Peaks, a mountain chain to the north, I encountered cilantro growing in the wild.

The property had stood vacant for many years before the farmworker movement bought it. Kern County had not been successful in selling the 187-acre property. There had been no offers to buy at the public auctions until a friendly Hollywood producer and writer by the name of Edward Lewis, made a bid for the tract of land. Because of the great hostility toward Cesar on the part of the growers in the county, it would never have been sold to him, and despite protests over the sale after discovering the purchaser's intent, it was too late. The deal had been struck.

As one of my early assignments as in-house counsel, I worked with former house counsel, Frank Dennison, on finalizing the transfer of the property to the National Farmworkers Service Center, Inc. It was accomplished at Cesar's insistence many years after the original transaction with Mr. Lewis, the proxy the movement had used to acquire it.

In early 1977, when I arrived at the La Paz community as in-house counsel, there were about two hundred people living there. That included some families and a few organizers who had been brought back from working in various cities around the country on the grape boycott. Thanks to the ALRA and Governor Brown who helped enact it, we had about 120 contracts in effect throughout the state, so they were busy times. The high number of contracts resulted from the fact that the UFW was winning over 80% of the ALRB-conducted representation elections. Among those living at La Paz the longest were *veteranos* Lupe Murguia and my good friend from the Azores who I nicknamed "*Porto Fino*," Modesto Gallo Winery striker, Mario Vargas. Stout and friendly, Mario is still at La Paz, standing guard.

One of the distinguishing features about La Paz was the Southern Pacific train that when headed east looped around the property, climbing toward what's called the Tehachapi Loop. The track was no longer used for passenger trains when we were in La Paz. That had stopped in 1971. The freight trains would pass through La Paz at all hours of the day and night. Also, Keene had one small combination restaurant and store called the Keene Cafe. It looked like any small country store and was built in 1920. Since the nearest town of Tehachapi was a 20-minute drive away, we would sometimes visit the Keene Cafe for a meal. But this was not too often as we only received $20 a week for food and personal items. Later, we ended up boycotting it for selling Coors beer. It is now owned by the farmworker movement.

Vickie came to join me in August. We were assigned one of the larger rooms in what had been the hospital and joined up with the vegetarian faction of the communal kitchens. There were four kitchens, and at the other end of the building was the "carnivorous kitchen," composed of meat-eaters and smokers. In each of the kitchens, dinner was eaten communally, and all took turns cooking. Ours was often visited by Cesar who would sometimes eat with us, or simply bring by celebrities or journalists on assignment.

Sometimes vegetarian meals can get boring, but the way we worked it out was to assign each person in the kitchen a day to cook. We had about ten people in the kitchen so each of us would cook once every two weeks. We didn't cook on weekends. Everyone was on their own then. One of the best cooks was an older woman named Rosie Cooperrider. She would help her husband, Verne, cook on his assigned day also, so we would have the benefit of having a Rosie home-cooked meal once a week. She made most things from scratch, including yogurt. Since Rosie was a hard act to follow, the cooking became a sort of competition among all of us, each trying to outdo the other for the best meal. And that's how we became the best and most popular kitchen in the "Hospital," which is what the building had been. Of course, there were times when the meal was not very good, but we gave thanks and ate it anyway, knowing that later in the week we would get a good Rosie meal.

I have other great memories of the four years based in La Paz. They include Cesar's birthday parties every March 31, community meetings on Friday nights, skits we performed at those meetings, preparing a full Thanksgiving dinner for the community when our regular cook took ill, Cesar's Saturday workdays in the organic community garden, pulling guard duty at the gate all night, climbing Three Peaks in the spring, and going for pizza in Tehachapi.

The baptisms of my niece Katrina Lopez, and Carlos Alcala and Ellen Egger's son, Tomás Eggers, also took place there, thanks to Father Ken Irrgang, the UFW chaplain at La Paz. I count them among my seven godchildren. There were several weddings, too. One that stands out was that of UFW organizer Larry and Annie Tramutola's Italian-style wedding. Larry and Annie had requested that no alcohol be served at their wedding, other than the wine served with the meal. In that regard, thanks to the wine companies up north that were under UFW contract, there was plentiful red wine to serve on what turned out to be a very warm day. Verne Cooperrider, who was in charge of the Union's new word-processing department, recruited a group of us to be the waiters.

We were to wear coats and ties, with a well-ironed red napkin draped over our left arms at all times. In our initial appearance, as we brought out the wine decanters, we sang *Funiculì Funiculà*, a song we had just learned "in the wings":

Listen! Listen! Echoes sound afar! Listen! Listen! Echoes sound afar! Funiculi funicula`, funiculi funicula`, Echoes sound afar! funiculi, funicula`!

Most large meetings, board meetings, and community celebrations were held in what was referred to as the North Unit. It was set apart a quarter mile from the main area of the compound, in what had been the children's ward. It had two large halls, a separate room where the board met, numerous rooms that were remodeled as law offices, and a conference room. The North Unit was one of the locations in La Paz that had its share of ghost stories dating back many years. It was said that in the basement one could hear children talking, laughing, or weeping, especially at night. Some years after my arrival, the legal department was moved to the basement after we outgrew the old guardhouse. Late one night, I heard what sounded like children playing on the floor above, while I worked alone in the basement. It was past ten and all the staff had left by 6:30 p.m. The hair on the nape of my hair stood on end. I went upstairs to take a look but saw no one at all in the building. Not wanting to frighten my staff, the following Monday I explained the sounds as the settling of the foundation.

During the first year I was in La Paz, it was expected of me, as the Union's house counsel, to attend the meetings of the UFW Executive Board. When Vickie arrived, her first assignment was to publish a bilingual President's Newsletter from Cesar to the workers. Cesar also asked her to attend the meetings. It was a thrill to watch the board members interacting first hand, sometimes laboring over difficult decisions that would have a monumental impact on the union. Not that Cesar, Dolores Huerta, Eliseo Medina, Richard Chavez, Jessica Govea, Marshall Ganz, Pete Velasco, Mack Lyons, and Gilbert Padilla always agreed on everything, but they all respected each other tremendously and it was apparent in the way they communicated. In every decision the Board made, the bottom line, was how it would impact the workers.

To improve the services being offered to the workers, Cesar and the Executive Board came up with the idea of sending some of the Union's volunteers to Mexico to study Spanish. The idea was to help them become better negotiators, administrators, and paralegals so they could more effectively serve the Union. It struck me as being quite similar to the two-year "*servicio social*" (social service) that university graduates in Mexico are required to perform before entering their chosen professions.

The program was set up to work as an exchange of services-for-lessons. Essentially, fifteen to twenty students traveled to the fishing hamlet of San Felipe, which lies at the northern coast of the Sea of Cortez in Baja California. Pete Moya, Director of Education for the new UFW schools, served as their resident teacher and coordinator. Vickie was also part of the group. The students resided in the homes of local families and volunteered on various community work projects.

Approximately three weeks into the program, I accompanied Cesar to Phoenix where we met with his friend Bill Soltero, Secretary-Treasurer of the Laborers Union in Arizona. A number of us traveled from La Paz: Cesar, Ramona Holguín, Marc Grossman, myself, and several of Cesar's bodyguards. We traveled in two cars, leaving La Paz very early in the morning and arriving in Phoenix by mid-day. The meetings with his old friend were relatively brief, but Cesar was pleased with the outcome and was in a jovial mood afterward.

Before we left Soltero's offices, Cesar asked me if I wanted to go to San Felipe to visit Vickie and the students. I thought at the time he might be teasing. We had already driven 500 miles to Phoenix, and a meeting was scheduled with workers and Union staff in North San Diego County that evening before our drive back home.

I said "sure," perhaps sounding somewhat incredulous.

Soon after, I heard him inform the rest of our group of the change in plans. I couldn't imagine how we would be able to fit this all in one day, but that was the pace Cesar kept on the road.

I wasn't in the lead car with Cesar on the way down, so I had no idea when, or with whom, arrangements were made for a Baja State police escort. When we crossed the border at Mexicali, two friendly *judiciales* (state police) greeted us and escorted our motorcade safely to San Felipe. One thing of note on the trip was that, like in our own California, Baja also had a saline lake near the border known as *Laguna Salada* (Salton Lake). Some geologists maintain that these two lakes are joined beneath the earth through a series of underground channels or rivers. Flourishing on the land above, on both sides of the border, are the same flora and fauna. Drawn boundaries are indeed among the inventions of mankind.

As we drove into the small village, I saw several children run up to the shoulders of the dirt road to greet us. They would disappear into the clouds of dust kicked up behind us, then reappear unfettered by the fleeting sandstorm. Their excitement lit us up, breaking the monotony of the long drive. Word of our visit had preceded us, for upon our arrival all the students were there to greet us. They were all very glad to see Cesar.

Over the next couple of hours, we ate with the students and met with some of the local officials. After discussing the Spanish educational program and the feasibility of future exchange programs, we bade farewell and resumed our trip to San Diego.

Once again, escorted by the two *judiciales*, we began our trip over the Sierra Pinta mountains northwest toward Ensenada from where we would travel north to Tijuana and then across the Mexico-US border into North San Diego County, a trip of some 300 miles.

Driving west with plenty of light, the sun had already started to set in front of us. After forty-five minutes driving over the mountains, we came upon a horrible multiple-car accident. It had just happened a short time before, as injured people lay strewn about the lanes and median divider. Nearby were some wrecked vehicles. Some were still smoldering from the damage. Our escorts pulled over and rushed into action, checking on the victims. We remained in our cars, waiting and watching.

A semi-truck, which was involved, appeared to have rear-ended two of the five vehicles now on and off the roadway, and the trucker and one other person were helping the most severely injured of those lying on the road. One of the *judiciales* joined them. One other victim had an open head wound and was bleeding profusely; she seemed lifeless. The scene was ghastly.

After a few minutes went by, one of the state *judiciales* returned and informed Cesar that they would have to stay behind and wait until other help arrived to take the injured. They suggested we drive on ahead, assuring us that we shouldn't have any problems, and so we drove on.

The sun cast its shadows over the entire roadway and a good part of the high, rocky, Sierra Pinta mountains. The winding road climbed steeply as we ventured ahead. Peering at the distant, barren mountaintops, I saw in my mind's eye the injured and thought that a couple of them appeared more dead than alive. No one spoke. I steered my thoughts to the meeting ahead of us.

After several miles of long, winding road, I saw a man swinging a smoky oil lantern in the distance. He signaled in our direction, standing just to the side of the road. Our guards, in radio contact with each other, passed on the order to stop and continued on.

We passed by the man and barely seconds passed when shots rang out behind us. As I turned and looked behind my shoulder, I saw that a vehicle sped behind us, leaving a tall cloud of dust. It was in hot pursuit. At first, David Valle, our driver, sped up, but then, perhaps seeing that the military vehicle behind us was rapidly approaching, he began to slow down. I caught his worried eyes in the rearview mirror.

In moments, they signaled us to pull off the road. Within seconds, a jeep loaded with *federale*s had us pull over, turn around, and head back to where the man with a lantern had stood. As we exited the highway, I noticed a group of soldiers gathered around a campfire. They were armed, their piercing gaze focused on us.

"*Federales*" are Mexican federal soldiers, mostly of poor and indigenous backgrounds, who come mainly from the southern states of Mexico. They are extremely loyal to their government and have a reputation for being able to put a bullet right through the middle of your forehead from ample distance. They proved their fierce loyalty to the government in 1968 when hundreds of students and union protestors were killed at their hands in Mexico City.

As a child, I had looked them right in the eyes when visiting Mexico City; their grim facial expressions had never shifted, and neither did these.

We were ordered out of our vehicles at gunpoint. *El Capitán* barked at his troops from his seat near the fire. In a funny sort of "Mexican John Wayne" drawl, he bellowed out orders for us to line up next to our cars. It's interesting how when one is stressed you notice things that even under dire circumstances can be quite humorous.

Since I have known Marc Grossman, press representative and speechwriter for Cesar, whenever he got nervous, he would twitch, and his eyes would role upward. His head would start to move from side to side like an old manual typewriter, rapidly from side to side, and Marc was known to type more than a hundred words per minute. For this reason, I think, the guards had nicknamed him "Radar," after the character on the TV show MASH. I caught a glimpse of him from one side and sure enough, here Marc was, doing the old typewriter routine for the *Capitán*.

As any military officer anywhere in the world would ask under these circumstances, the first question we were asked was "Why did you not stop when signaled?" Our inquisitor was clearly angered by what he perceived to be a blatant defiance of his "*autoridad*." Behind a soft veneer, authority is sacrosanct in Mexico, and this did not look good. Our faces showed it.

I was standing next to Cesar who nudged me and in a calm voice said,

"Marco, you do the talking."

The campfire lit *El Capitán's* grubby face with an orange glow, partially revealing his five-day beard and his dangling toothpick, which he adeptly moved from one side of his mouth to the other. He exchanged cursory glances with each of us in the line-up before he stood up and slowly made his way closer.

"*Muestren sus identificaciones, todos!*" (Show your identifications, all of you!) the *Capitán* demanded.

His commanding military cadence broke the relative tension for me. I stiffened up and began communicating with Mexican authority. It was time to perform.

After a thorough visual inspection he instinctively walked over to Cesar. One of his men made his way down the line looking at our identifications.

"*De donde vienen?*" (Where do you come from?)

I answered, "*Somos de los Estados Unidos, de California. Y él es César Chávez, líder sindicalista de los campesinos*" (We're from the United States, from California. And he is Cesar Chavez, farmworker labor leader.)

I looked at Cesar, who was looking at the *Capitán*, waiting for some kind of reaction as I explained to him who Cesar was and that we were all union volunteers with the movement. I got the distinct feeling that this was not making any sort of impression at all, or, worse yet, he was starting to think we were *agitadores* (agitators.)

His eyebrow arched sluggishly,

"*Y que hacen por acá?*" (And what brings you here?)

I explained why we had come to San Felipe and about the practical Spanish-learning program and the students we had just visited. I also told him of our Baja State police escort which we, unfortunately, lost at the scene of a collision a few miles back. Judging by the way the *Capitán* started to look at us, I thought I was finally beginning to make some progress.

"*Esculquen los carros,*" (Search the cars) *El Capitán* ordered his men.

Now that our identities had been scrutinized, the soldiers began searching our cars. No problem, I thought. What could they find? Our notebooks? Cesar's books and Union literature? Cesar was a voracious and diverse reader. When traveling long distances he would often prefer to read instead of gazing at the landscape he'd seen so many times before. For reading at night, he had a clip-on light, which could be seen reflected off the car windows as the odometer clicked away the miles.

As the *Capitán* walked over to the other car to question them, I had started to become mesmerized by the Spanish murmurs off in the distance and the flames of the campfire, dancing slowly under the clear evening sky.

I came to myself when I heard "*pistolas.*"

"*¿Pistolas?*"

The word "guns" reverberated in my momentarily vacuous mind. Cesar and I exchanged quick glances, not unlike that any attorney and client would in open court.

"Guns where?" I inadvertently let out.

I turned to look at the bustle at one of our car's trunks. One of the soldiers had pulled out two handguns. Looking in the *Capitán's* direction, he raised them at eye level as one proudly would a trophy. They belonged to Cesar's bodyguards.

Now what?

One learns early on in life that in awkward moments such as these, the best one can do is to look innocent. It really doesn't matter how you do it, just do it; and the sooner, the better. Well, I looked over to Cesar and sure enough — he looked very innocent; and I, I must confess, looked very perplexed. Were we two sides of the same coin, variations on the same theme?

Despite this most recent discovery and turn of events, I felt confident. Hell, what could they do, shoot us? I wasn't about to ask.

"You are all under arrest," the *Capitán* said, as he walked away from us.

There was no need to ask why we were being detained. I well knew that unlike in the United States, where the right to bear arms is protected by the Constitution, in Mexico that is not the case. It has something to do with her revolutions, insurrections, and instability; the same instability *el Capitán* was sworn to protect against.

I asked the captain where we were being taken.

"*Para Ensenada—a la carcel,*" (to the Ensenada jail) he said, in a now more respectful tone.

"*Todos a sus coches.*" (All of you to your cars.)

Had the guns bestowed upon us more respect? It sure seemed that way. He now even sounded a bit like a tourist guide —

"*¡Vamonos!*" (Let's go!)

Whatever the reason for the captain's change in attitude, I found solace in the thought that at least we were not going to be shot and buried out there somewhere in the desolate La Pinta range.

Cesar gave me a "good job" kind of look and off we went to the Ensenada jail.

Leaving the La Pinta range, I now rode in Cesar's car, now being driven by a *federal,* courtesy of the Mexican government. Sitting in the back with Cesar, we talked for the entire one and one-half-hour drive to the jail, as always, alternating between English and Spanish. Not a word was said by the *federal,* in the presence of whom we did not broach any sensitive subjects.

Our caravan was now up to five vehicles, two civilian and three military, a worthy entourage. We sped through the mountains, then down through a valley and many curves until arriving in Ensenada.

When I was a boy, I went with my uncle Yb Quezada Núñez and other family members for a weekend in this small coastal town in Baja California. We stayed at his friend's ranch on the outskirts of town, situated between a Catholic seminary and a small military post. On our mornings there we were awoken by two very loud, contrasting ritual styles. Before dawn each day, at the pre-dawn of day, the pealing of church bells could be heard from one direction. Then from the other direction, as if the result of some church/state coordination, came the sound of a bugle reveille. If that didn't wake you up, the roosters certainly would. At dusk, the ritual would repeat, without the roosters.

In between the ghost stories, in high demand among us kids, my uncle told us a very interesting story about something that happened after he served as a staff sergeant in the U.S. Army. He saw combat in the Philippine Islands in 1944, receiving a Purple Heart for wounds received in battle. Like my mother, he was born in Dawson, New Mexico. When the miners went out on strike, which my grandfather and his eldest sons all joined, and their economic situation turned for the worse, grandfather Agustín Quezada moved the family to Cananea, in the northern Mexican State of Sonora. As soon as they arrived, my grandfather registered my Mom, *tía* Hortencia, and *tío* Yb as Mexican citizens born in the exterior. My mother, therefore, not only had dual citizenship, but was equally grateful for, and loyal, to both nations. None felt conflicted in the least.

After his honorable discharge, my uncle Yb went into business and was one of the first modern tortilla manufacturers in Los Angeles. He was a very successful businessman and active in many service clubs. While in the Lions Club, he met a group of retired army and naval officers. After socializing with them, he was asked, in private, to join in their plan to invade and seize control of the entire Baja Peninsula. I listened, totally astounded, to his exciting story of intrigue. I looked at him with eyes and mouth agape.

"Why didn't you do it, *tío*?!" I asked.

The lesson uncle Yb taught me is one that I carry to this day. He explained to me the unique responsibility of dual citizenship and the respect a nation should have for the boundaries of its neighbors.

"So, what did you tell them?"

"Well, I smiled at them," he said as he looked intently at us with wide eyes, "… looked 'em straight in the eyes and said, 'why? You already live in occupied territory!'"

Not completely understanding why he laughed, we were nevertheless affected by his warm laughter and laughed along with him. Years later, when I was a law student, I visited him in Los Angeles. I heard him tell a couple of his white business friends the same lesson about living in occupied territory. I understood now as they laughed with him. He had charisma. These memories flooded my mind as we entered Ensenada. I thought of uncle Yb who had just recently passed away, and I smiled.

I looked out my window as we turned down a dark cobblestone street. The station was brightly lit by the powerful halogen lamps one would see at a state fair. There were squad cars parked outside with a number of policemen milling around, some of them having their dinner at a taco stand set up in front of the station. I imagined them talking about their calls and conquests and wondered if our next inquisitor was among them. Their attention immediately turned to our caravan pulling in. Once more we would be scrutinized.

We exited our cars to the mixed aromas of sea breeze, tacos, and exhaust fumes, and were quickly escorted into the jail. There was a changing of guards as our custody was passed on to the local police. I hoped they would be more knowledgeable about Cesar and all his good work "*al Norte*," as some Mexicans refer to their neighbor to the north.

Mexican culture is very hierarchal in these matters. There is a lot of waiting involved, as one is passed along from one level of public servant to the next. Of course, the entire process can be sped up in proportion to the "*mordida*" (bribe). If one gives a handsome gratuity at the start of one's official visit, the length of the process is diminished considerably, again depending on the amount of the *mordida*.

Cesar never carried money with him, and even if he did, he would not have paid. Much to our surprise, we didn't have to wait very long before the *Comandante* himself came from out of his office, pristinely dressed, professional, and courteous.

"*Buenas noches señores, y señorita*." (Good evening gentlemen, and ma'am.)

Cesar motioned for me to speak again. Before I spoke, Cesar whispered to me,

"Ask him to please call their Senator, my friend."

Now I knew we stood on firmer ground. I exchanged greetings with the *Comandante* and respectfully began telling him our story. After I'd given him the same spiel I'd wasted on the surly captain, I nonchalantly added that he only had to call his Senator, who would vouch for us. My eyes caught those of the *Capitán,* standing across the room from the *Comandante,* looking worried that he might lose his score. With a furrowed forehead, he now appeared pensive and annoyed.

Cesar handed me the Senator's phone number, which I gave to the *Comandante.*

"Me perdonan por favor. Enseguida regreso." (You'll excuse me, please. I will return shortly.)

He dismissed himself and went back into his office, the *Capitán* following behind. Perhaps, as Captain Renault said in the movie, *Casablanca,* he had not rounded up the "usual suspects." But then, why should he have been worried? Ultimately, he knew he answered to a higher authority.

As we nervously waited, an officer asked if we would like anything to drink. Cesar asked for and was quickly given water. I could hear the *Comandante* carrying on what sounded like a friendly conversation in his office. Then, after about five minutes, the office door opened and the *Comandante* came back out, his eyes turned downward. Reaching out to shake Cesar's hand the *Comandante* said,

"*Sr. Chávez, me da mucho gusto conocerlo. El Señor Senador le envía sus más cordiales saludos.*" (Mr. Chavez, it is a true pleasure meeting you. The Senator conveys to you his most cordial greetings.)

Cesar and I thanked him for his kind courtesies. We all shook hands and Cesar and I returned to the car. We would still make the staff meeting in Carlsbad. We were all exhausted after the hour or so we were there. But my day, I soon discovered, was not yet over. Cesar told me his guards were too burned out to continue driving and asked whether I would mind taking over.

"Not at all Cesar."

We arrived at La Paz at daybreak. We all exchanged goodnights, then went off in separate directions to rest after our grueling journey.

After about three hours of sleep, I went to my office in the basement directly below Cesar's. I heard Cesar above me in his office and no sooner had I sat at my desk when he called me on the intercom and asked me to come up to see him. He was alone and ready to start a new day.

"That was quite an adventure, wasn't it?"

"Yes, it sure was," I said. "I've got to tell you; I was a bit worried out there."

He nodded his head. We went over some of the highlights of our trip and other items for the day, after which he thanked me for having spoken up in Baja.

"You're welcome," I replied, as I walked toward the door, preparing to leave. Then, I heard him ask from behind me,

"Marco, can we get the guns back?" I stopped dead in my tracks, turned to face him, and said,

"No Cesar. I don't think so."

"No, right?"

"Nope."

We both exchanged the same innocent looks we'd given the *Capitán.* I was getting to know Cesar's sense of humor.

Unbeknownst to us, when we were apprehended at La Pinta range on September 26, 1977, the federal government had been put on full-alert due to the fact that October 2nd marked the anniversary of the tragic Mexican student revolt in Mexico City in 1968. There had been reports of potential guerilla activities throughout Mexico, including in the La Pinta range. This was confirmed to me months after by a contact in the Mexican Foreign Ministry.

22.

While living in La Paz during the seventies, I received a call from the FBI, informing us that there was a contract out on Cesar's life. With four UFW supporters martyred through the years, we considered any such information to be extremely important. We had been given the name of a suspect who was employed by the Southern Pacific on the short haul from Bakersfield to the Mojave Desert. La Paz was on this route, and we were gearing up for a general strike, so this was particularly alarming. As soon as I received this report, I immediately went out to the North Unit where Cesar was holding a meeting. I entered discreetly, trying my best to get his attention. He called a break so we could speak privately, but as I told him he seemed remarkably unaffected. It occurred to me that for him this might have been business as usual. When I told him that we had been given an address and phone number for the suspect, he turned abruptly toward me and with a genuine look of shock asked,

"What?"

"Yes, Cesar. The man lives on Kentucky Street in Bakersfield; we have an address." With that bit of information, Cesar visibly perked up and directed me to investigate. I assured him I would and left him to his meeting.

Early the following morning, I left for Bakersfield. I told the staff that I was going to the Kern County Law Library to return a couple of special legal reference books as a favor to the librarian who hesitantly lent them to me. This wasn't false, but they weren't actually due for another week.

As I started out, Cesar wished me good luck and asked that I not take any risks.

"I'll call you later, from Bakersfield?"

"Please do," he said, and I was gone.

The morning was cold, and as I descended Highway 58, the Tule fog made it seem like I was above the clouds. Having been raised in Bakersfield, I knew the risks and peculiarities of the

"silent killer," as some called it. During a winter day such as this, the fog would blanket the entire San Joaquin Valley for days on end, keeping the temperature bone-chilling cold. I was hyper-aware of train crossings and semis barreling through. I had a very close call in the fog when I was a teenager.

The address I was looking for was located near the intersection of Kentucky and Baker Streets, in what was once known as Kern City, now a part of Bakersfield. Many years earlier, the area had been established by the Southern Pacific Railroad. Buildings of a former train station still stood, as well as a small, but still functioning, railroad facility. Baker Street had been a busy business hub when I was a kid back in 1958. I recall catching the last Christmas parade held there before it was moved to Chester Avenue in the downtown area.

Looking back on that day, I realize how uncanny it was that I was investigating a lead to a suspect who was employed by Southern Pacific, having lived in a former Southern Pacific town, a company that made millions of dollars hauling the world's supply of grapes and other fruits and vegetables from out of the heart of California.

As I got near to the address, the fog was beginning to lift, thanks to the sun slowly burning through the chilled air. I was aware that since I had left Bakersfield in the early seventies, this area had been somewhat overtaken by heroin addicts and drug dealers. During this hour though, the streets were abandoned by drug dealers, making way for hard-working people and students trudging their way to school. I would walk the short way to Kentucky Street and then knock at the door of a man I did not know yet. Despite this, I was entirely focused. I know I was a lawyer by education and training, but the niceties of "due process" and "presumption of innocence" had taken a back seat, not that I blindly believed the FBI. We later learned that beginning with J. Edgar Hoover, the agency had been actively spying on Cesar and the UFW from its beginning. Not wanting to look conspicuous, I tossed my portfolio in the trunk, grabbing only my notes of my discussion with Bakersfield FBI agent Logan the day before and my micro-cassette recorder. There wasn't much I had to go on, but we had actually been given more than expected. At the end of my conversation with agent Logan, I was left with the impression that they would not be conducting much of an investigation, something Cesar and I were not at all surprised about. The way we left it with them was that we would share whatever information we obtained, and they would reciprocate. We weren't holding our breath.

Before walking up Baker, I bundled up and locked the car. It took me all of five minutes to walk the short distance to Kentucky Street, where I waited to cross Baker to what turned out to be a rather tidy, though very old building, west of the intersection.

At first glance, the buildings looked uninhabited, with the front windows shuttered by dark-yellowish Venetian blinds, or heavy lace curtains of many years gone past. I stopped in front of the address and looked up the steep stairway for a moment.

Just as I started up the stairs an elderly gentleman exited the building next door looking only straight ahead of him and toward the morning sun.

"Sir, excuse me, can you please tell me if a Mr. Stuart lives at this address?" Without so much as acknowledging me, he simply called out,

"Speak to Mrs. Harding. She should be able to help you."

He dashed down onto the sidewalk without breaking his pace.

I came to the dark, heavy doors in front of me and knocked. After a few minutes of not hearing anything stirring inside, I knocked again, this time louder than the first.

Still nothing.

I turned away from the door and looked down the street when from inside there came the sound of a woman's hard heels. A stout woman peered out from the curtains and then spoke to me through the gap allowed by the security chain.

"How may I help you, sir?"

"Good morning, ma'am. Mrs. Harding, is it?"

"Who'd like to know?"

"I'm sorry, my name is Marco Lopez. I have been given this address as belonging to Mr. Stuart. Does he live here?"

She squinted some while raising an eyebrow.

"No, this is not his house. This is my boarding home, and he's one of my boarders. I have seven."

"May I speak with him?"

"Well, I would see no harm in that, but you see, Mr. Stuart is not here. He works for the railroad and is away for a few days. You're free to leave him a message if you'd like."

I paused and answered, "I'd rather come back if that's okay with you?"

With a now friendlier voice, Mrs. Harding said, "Sure."

It was back to La Paz, but I'd call Cesar from the Arizona Café.

Don Toribio was the owner of the Arizona Café. I had known him since I was a kid. Mom had convinced him to buy her products for his busy restaurant. Back then, it was just off Baker Street. He inherited the café from his wife. It was her mother who had brought the café's famous *chile verde* recipe north from the state of Michoacán, Mexico. The matriarch died at the age of 107. He was now a good friend and poker buddy of my cousin, Edmundo, who had recently taken over as new co-owner of *La Bonita*. Since I had moved away from Bakersfield, we rarely saw each other, but it was always a treat. He called out my usual order to the cook motioning that he would come right back to talk.

"*Que pués mi Lic., que lo trae por acá?*" (What's going on with my Lic.?)

"*Ando investigando a uno de sus vecinos.*" (I am investigating one of your neighbors.)

He put on a classic poker face while turning his attention to a customer who had just walked in.

"*¿Y cómo está su mamá? La Bonita.*" (And how is your mother?)

"*Está bien Don Toribio, ya en Los Angeles, con mi hermanita, Patricia.*" (She's fine Don Toribio. She's now in Los Angeles with my baby sister.)

"*Si, pues. Nos dejó aquí abandonados,*" (Well, yes. She left us abandoned here,) he said humorously.

He excused himself as he returned to his business. Since the beginning of the movement, he had been an ardent supporter of Cesar, Dolores, and the UFW. The cafe's walls were decorated with blown-up, iconic photographs of Mexican revolutionaries, Emiliano Zapata and Francisco "Pancho" Villa with his *Dorados*, so I felt right at home here, and knew that I could treat it as such.

I phoned La Paz to give Cesar my report, but instead I spoke with his secretary, Esther Winterrowd, who told me that he had been called to a meeting. I told her that our suspect was not home and was working on a Southern Pacific train somewhere. She expressed concern but quickly added that security had been beefed up in La Paz and that there was to be a community meeting in the evening. Lastly, she told me that Cesar had asked that I return to La Paz right away.

Over my *chile verde* and coffee I informed Don Toribio about my investigation. The Arizona had picked up its usual pace by the time I left. I said goodbye to my old friend, who simply nodded and told me he'd keep his eyes and ears open.

I whispered to him, "*Ya sabe Don Toribio, bajo de ala,*" (You know Don Toribio, on the q.t.) and nodded back at him.

Upon my return from Bakersfield, Esther told me that security had been bolstered. I knew that during dangerous periods such as these the number of people assigned to guard the property more than tripled. On this particular day, it was Elizar Vásquez who was manning the gate. He was one of *los veteranos*, a seasoned member of Cesar's personal security detail, and the best person to be there. The UFW was not unlike other organizations, which can evolve into an entity unto themselves, the minds of all melding into one. It is created and reinforced by communal living, sharing in an overall goal. It is bound by loyalty to both cause and leadership. When one is threatened, especially someone like Cesar, all feel it.

The weekly community meeting was generally dedicated to filling in staff on UFW news from throughout California and the nation, the introduction of new staff members, departmental reports, and the usual agenda items. Today, we would be addressing the FBI's tip regarding Mr. Stuart.

Chris Hartmire opened up the meeting, then Cesar gave a summary of what was going on, including some details of my investigation.

There were a few gasps at hearing that the man worked for Southern Pacific as a brakeman and passed through La Paz regularly. Cesar then turned the meeting over to Esther's husband, Kent Winterrowd. Kent was an overall congenial but serious-minded former cop, originally from Ohio. He was also Richard Chavez's golfing partner and barber to Cesar and most of La Paz.

Kent and a couple of *veteranos* had prepared a four-point security plan for La Paz and Cesar. It was concise, professional, and called for the participation of the entire community.

The present small security staff would be assisted by all those capable of performing any one of the necessary duties: manning the front gate, covering Cesar's home and fenced perimeter, guarding Cesar individually, the vehicular surveillance of the La Paz property, etc. We were all asked to sign a volunteer list and schedule sheet before leaving the meeting. I signed up for the front gate.

Despite its claustrophobic confines, the small heater we had in the front gate security booth didn't have much effect on these cold night shifts.

A few days into our security regimen, Kent called to ask me if I could cover for him. I would be with Cesar from six o'clock in the evening until his day ended, at which time a regular guard would then escort him home for the evening. Kent informed me that although the start time was firm, Cesar's days could go until late before his labor was done.

Since I was so accustomed to hearing Cesar's bustling about through the ceiling, I was also used to his typical schedule. Throughout the day I would hear the sounds of steps, moving of chairs, and him calling out instructions or holding meetings. There were also long lapses of time that filled his absence. I knew it was time for my shift during the six-o'clock lull, so I headed up to his office, took a seat, and remained inconspicuous as he and Esther finished scheduling meetings.

"Oh good, you're here. Kent told me you were covering for him. Sorry for the inconvenience."

"Not at all, Cesar."

"Thanks. I have a couple of meetings left here, so you're welcomed to join me, or take that desk and do your work. It's up to you."

"If it's okay, I'll just stay out here and review some documents I got from Salinas legal. But if you need anything, just holler."

Esther could sense that I was feeling a little insecure about my first security detail assignment, so she kindly said to me,

"Good luck tonight, Marco."

I made a quick visual sweep of all windows and doors, then sat down to catch up on some memos and correspondence. As the time passed, staff would enter, acknowledge me, and go in or out of Cesar's office. It was filled with old solid wooden furniture, bookshelves filled to capacity, memorabilia, numerous formal recognitions, and a photograph taken of him breaking his fast with Robert Kennedy in 1968. A couple of times Cesar checked in on me via intercom. It was around nine o'clock when Cesar and his last group bid goodnight. He placed some items in a bag and walked out happy his day was over, or so I thought.

"That wasn't too bad, was it?"

"Not at all," I said, shaking my head slightly.

"Good. Now I just need to make a couple of visits at the Hospital on my way home."

The Hospital referred to the large building behind the administration building where some of us lived. Cesar's visits this evening were with two volunteers: a farmworker from Salinas who had just come on board and a long-term boycott supporter and clerical volunteer from New York City. Both were pleasantly surprised that Cesar himself would personally welcome them. Cesar's energy was very motivating, but what I had initially not realized was that he was equally receptive to the positive energy of those he came in contact with. It was a powerful chemistry.

Cesar's long evening was finally over and we both walked down the long hallway to the swinging doors that led outside into the night. The tempestuous wind howled at us. Cesar and I made our way up the path leading to his home. In front of the community kitchen building on our right, I caught sight of a tall, silhouetted figure standing near the bushes by the Murguia's home. The dim lighting made it difficult to recognize the mysterious person, who was not coming up on my mental Rolodex.

Thinking caution was the better course to take, I placed my left hand on Cesar's shoulder and quickly guided him toward the other end of the shrubbery. We both took a semi-crouched position there, with Cesar hidden on my left side, and I only partially hidden — all the while maintaining sight of the black figure, now with both his hands in the pockets of what appeared to be a long trench coat. We had stayed hidden two or three minutes when I felt Cesar gently tugging on my jacket. I turned and saw him looking at me, intently...

"*¿Marco?*"

"*...¿Si?*"

"*¿Traes cuete*?" (Do you have a weapon?)

"*No.*"

At that very moment, I saw Cesar looking slightly upward.

"Bhew," I heard him say...sounding let down, but not as let down as I felt.

No one had ever explained to me that I should, or could even, pack a weapon. I was completely crestfallen, feeling I had let Cesar down. Then to compound the embarrassment, after some moments had passed one of our volunteers drove by and picked up the mystery shadow and I got a clear look at him. I said to Cesar,

"It's Pat Bonner."

He didn't respond.

Bonner was a kind, gentle, real prince of a man, who had left the Jesuit order to volunteer full-time for the Union. I first met Pat when I was transferred to Irwindale while working on the LA boycott under LeRoy Chatfield in 1970.

It turned out Pat had come up from Los Angeles for the weekend to participate in some planning sessions. I waved to him as he passed by in the guard's car.

When we got to Cesar's gate, I handed him off to Jorge Rivera who then walked him the short distance to his door.

A lone light shone from inside. Cesar was home safe. It was past eleven o'clock.

Some days later I confided in my older brother, Florencio, who empathized. He excused himself and when he returned, handed me a leather, zippered pouch. Inside was a black .38 Smith & Wesson. I never had to use it.

On February 10, 1979, twenty-two days into a bitter Imperial Valley vegetable strike, Rufino Contreras, 28, and other UFW strikers walked into a lettuce field owned by Mario Saikhon. Their aim was simply to talk about the strike with a crew of scabs. Then, three, armed company foremen opened fire. Rufino was shot in the face and fell face-down in a muddy row. His father, Lorenzo, brother Jose Luis, and other Saikhon strikers tried to aid Rufino, but they were kept at bay by continuing gunfire. Finally, the sheriff's deputies arrived and called an ambulance. Rufino died in the hospital. Regardless of whether the strikers walked into, or rushed the field in question, it is clear it was done without first using "*submarinos*" to determine whether anyone in that particular field was armed.

The next day, Cesar's wife, Helen, accompanied members of Rufino's family to tell his young wife, Rosa, that her husband was dead. Through her profound grief, Rosa described him as a kind and gentle husband and father who always put his family first. Rosa, who had recently suffered severe burns from an incident at home was heavily bandaged and wheelchair-bound, went to see her husband's body at a funeral home with Helen at her side. As Rosa was leaving the hospital, she said to Rufino,

"*Vete tranquilo, mi amor, yo cuidare a tus hijos.*" (Go in peace, my love, I will take care of your children.)

Services were held for Rufino in Calexico on February 14, 1979. Once more, the black and white UFW bereavement flags flew for a Union martyr, this time in Imperial County.

In his moving eulogy, Cesar asked, "What is the worth of a man? What is the worth of a farmworker? Rufino, his father, and brother together gave the company twenty years of their labor. They were faithful workers who helped build up the wealth of their boss and helped build up the wealth of his ranch. What was their reward for their service and their sacrifice? When they petitioned for a more just share of what they themselves produced, when they spoke out against the injustice they endured, the company answered them with bullets; the company sent hired guns to quiet Rufino Contreras. Capital and labor together produce the fruit of the land. But what really counts is labor: the human beings who torture their bodies, sacrifice their youth and numb their spirits to produce this great agricultural wealth—a wealth so vast that it feeds all of America and much of the world. And yet the men, women, and children who are the flesh and blood of this production often do not have enough to feed themselves…In that sense, Rufino is not dead. Wherever farmworkers organize, stand up for their rights, and strike for justice, Rufino Contreras is with them."

Rufino Contreras became one of four men and one woman who

lost their lives striking on behalf of the UFW.

At the beginning of March 1979, I drove up to Salinas from the Imperial Valley where we had been wrapping up the first phase of the lettuce strike that would eventually move north to Salinas. The Union had a major mobilization effort going on in the vegetable industry, and it had all started with the winter harvest in Imperial County. After a couple of months, the strikers and organizers arrived in Salinas for the harvest there.

The Union organized a march into Salinas by the farmworkers to publicize their strike. We assembled on the grounds of a public school behind the UFW field office in Salinas. I wanted to pick Cesar's brain regarding pressing issues I was confronting with the representation of strikers arrested and charged criminally stemming from the strike in the Imperial Valley I had discovered early on that the best time to have Cesar focus on departmental issues was when he was marching, but because of Cesar's dark mood when we started, this march would prove different.

As we headed toward downtown Salinas, we heard the news outlets estimate that over 5,000 people were marching with Cesar. Although chanting was going on behind us, the marchers at the front were eerily quiet, as if in a vacuum, mirroring Cesar's mood. We proceeded up Alisal Street and approached a railroad underpass when suddenly two Monterey County Sheriff's vehicles raced down the right shoulder of the road. They came to an abrupt stop kicking up massive dust clouds. The deputies quickly exited their Broncos and ran toward the front of the line. Those of us surrounding Cesar became more anxious and alert. I instinctively looked over my shoulder attempting to figure out what the hell was coming down. Then, one of the deputies broke from his group and ran directly toward Cesar, who was shoulder-to-shoulder on my left.

"Mr. Chavez!" the deputy yelled.

As the deputy continued toward Cesar, my first instinct was to bolt from my position, but I was quickly overwhelmed by a powerful force equally uncanny. When he got to within three feet of me, I outstretched my right hand toward the deputy. The deputy went limp, stunned and disoriented. This precise moment was captured by Associated Press photographer, Paul Sakuma, and is the photograph on the cover of this book.

We continued marching and the deputies retreated as quickly as they had arrived. When I focused back on Cesar, his facial expression revealed he was a bit shaken.

A couple of minutes later Cesar handed me the subpoena dropped by the deputy. One of the marchers in front of us had handed it to Cesar, who in turn handed it to me and said,

"Marco, you quashed the subpoena."

As we continued our march, Cesar's facial expression slowly eased to normal. The disturbing incident had not turned violent, or deadly. We had used restraint which, given the circumstances, had not been easy. By the time our march arrived at Hartnell College, Cesar was

back to his fighting form, and we had a resoundingly successful rally before thousands of workers.

23.

Months earlier, Cesar had shared his philosophy of volunteerism with me, one not shared by all of the Union's leadership. He told me of its evolution and how he had modeled it after his early reading, principally the writing of Mahatma Gandhi. From Cesar's perspective, anyone in a position of leadership should live as simply as those whom they are leading, even if it required voluntary poverty.

Therefore, all of the Union's full-time staff were volunteers, including Cesar and all the members of the Executive Board, receiving $5.00 per week and room and board, which in the boycott cities often meant seeking donations for housing and food from supporters. The only staff who had ever received a salary were professionals: doctors and lawyers. This had been true since the beginning days of the union. I told Cesar that although I held no firm belief one way or another about volunteerism, I found it uncomfortable working in a system with both volunteers and paid employees. I also told him that I appreciated the $600 per month I was earning as a lawyer.

Cesar and I had several discussions involving other subjects, such as an attorney's role not only in unions but also in "the movement," and society in general. I had realized early on that some allies and supporters criticized Cesar for his involvement in any causes other than unionizing. Cesar sincerely believed that the plight of all poor people and the foundation of the Union were interconnected. Causes also helped in garnering support for the Union; and who could doubt that?

There were internal struggles within the Union over the years. Yet, to say that it was money alone that was at the root of the conflict within the UFW in the late 1970s, would be simplistic and inaccurate. A clash on the Union's Executive Board erupted over the direction the UFW would take after the passage of the ALRA in 1975. Some board members wanted a traditional business union, concentrating on wages, hours, and benefits for its members. Cesar's vision for the UFW was more transformational. Of course, he knew that the union had to produce economic progress for its members, but he also envisioned the UFW as leading a broad movement not only of farmworkers, but including a burgeoning community of Latino working families and other poor people as well. As in the practice of nonviolence in the 1960s, Cesar's vision prevailed then too, although critics still condemn him for it.

In the late 1970s, Cesar reached out to renowned Management-By-Objectives (MBO) guru, Peter Drucker. The Claremont professor readily agreed to meet with Cesar after which evolved a warm friendship and collaboration on how Drucker's management techniques, though intended primarily for corporations, could be applied to a union-in-transition, such as the UFW. Cesar not only had us read from Drucker's books, he also used MBO techniques in many of our meetings. He wanted input from all of us as to what the purpose of the UFW ought to be. Cesar was sincere in his effort to encourage us to determine the direction we should take, yet he was immediately ridiculed by his opponents within the Union. Some even said that the concept of deciding the purpose of an organization was "corporatist" with no relevance to a union. Despite this kind of ignorance, cynicism, and rancor, Cesar forged ahead.

When I look back upon Cesar's life, and the role I played within the movement, inevitably I recall those who fought him from within. For those not part of the movement in the late 1970s and early 1980s, it may be difficult to imagine that, among the many battles Cesar fought, those fought within the Union itself were among the fiercest.

Consider the Union's middle-class lawyers who came to believe that their way of life was superior to that of the volunteerism espoused by Cesar and the Union's leadership. They had asked for raises for the lawyers and salaries for para-legals. Among these was Cohen, the Union's veteran general counsel whose quick wit and sharp mind were influential in recruiting me. Cohen influenced me to become a lawyer, but Chavez inspired me to use my powers for the farmworker movement.

By 1979, Cesar had expressed alarm at the number of decisions being made by the legal department without Board input, and he felt he had lost control of the department. Cesar was emphatic at one of the board meetings,

"No one knows what all those lawyers are doing up there in Salinas. Legal policies are being implemented by Jerry, and we on the Board only find out after the fact."

The lines were being drawn about the issue of lawyer salaries, with Cohen-Ganz in one corner, and Chavez-Huerta in the other; true heavy-weights, the four of them. The UFW Board finally decided, after intense debate, that there would be no salaries paid to non-lawyers. It was also decided that the entire legal department would be transferred from Salinas to the headquarters in La Paz. Almost immediately, the meeting we had anticipated was called. Jerry asked Cesar to come meet with his legal department at their offices in downtown Salinas. Cesar asked me to attend with him, which I did.

Through the past months, I had observed the effects of stress caused by a deteriorating attorney-client relationship on Cesar, as well as on Cohen and his cadre of lawyers. From my point of view, the tumor would need to be extracted if the patient was to live.

We arrived at the legal department's offices, located on the second floor of a late 1880s building on West Gavilan Street. It was early in 1979. There was an ambiance of claustrophobia, as the heavy oak and glass door sealed Cesar and I inside with all of Cohen's department.

Crowded in the room were Cohen's lawyers, who comprised his legal department. Cesar and I sat side-by-side, and I closely observed each of the lawyers while taking mental notes.

Although Jerry opened the meeting, Sandy Nathan was the first to address the issues at hand. Next was Tom Dalzell, who had become a lawyer through the State Bar's apprenticeship program under the tutelage of Cohen and Nathan. Throughout the rest of the meeting, Nathan and Dalzell were the most vocal of the group. Cesar was subjected to the most scathing, verbal assault I have ever witnessed. In the confines of the law offices the angry insults rang out,

"Son-of-a-bitch!"

"Fucker!"

"Fucking asshole!"

The dark mood hung heavy like formaldehyde on an autopsy table. I imagined being on the most contentious of picket lines, but there was no comparison. For one thing, these were people who had for years dedicated themselves to the plight of the farmworker. They had gone up against the toughest attorneys and law firms in the state and won great legal victories for the Union. And yet, here they were, some yelling the worst obscenities, epithets, and accusations at the top of their lungs. The scene was surreal. It bordered on the absurd.

From time to time, I would look over at Cesar, who did not say a word. It was a reality check for me to see him in the thick of this ambush, seemingly unaffected. He remained expressionless, appearing centered and contained. I began to wonder whether racism was not at the root of this ambush. After all, none of them would have ever subjected the growers or their lawyers to such hateful behavior.

To think that attorneys would turn against their client in such a vile manner was mind-boggling.

Yet Cesar stayed above it all, thinking perhaps that it was cathartic for them or that it would pass soon enough. His advice given to me when I joined the Union echoed in my mind, "Never get involved in a pissing contest with a skunk." And here was Cesar, demonstrating it superbly. Though Jerry remained silent throughout, I knew well enough that he had orchestrated the entire confrontation. He was as much a political animal as was Cesar, and a Svengali of sorts to his staff.

After approximately an hour, maybe more, Cohen's lawyers were either burned out or ran out of things to say. All that was left was an uneasy silence about the room. I looked at Cesar, and he gave me a slight nod. I took that to be my cue, so I looked at Cohen and said,

"We'll be needing a full inventory of all the cases."

Cesar and I then stood up and left the room without a word. As we walked out of the old building onto Gavilan Street, Cesar and I walked silently down the sidewalk into the cool Salinas breeze. In my mind, I visualized the move of the legal department to the UFW headquarters 300 miles away; furniture, equipment, hundreds of law books, and dozens of filing cabinets. I thought to myself, "Damn, the move and all will be easy, compared to what Cesar and I just went through."

I was pensive when Cesar's car came up to the curb with a guard, Marc Grossman, and Paul Chavez, Cesar's son. Cesar was due elsewhere that evening and the many questions I had for him would have to wait. As the car drove off, Cesar lowered his window, "Marco, I really appreciate you coming with me." I nodded and waved as they drove off.

Now, after having freely expressed their hostility against Cesar, there was no longer any chance of a reconciliation. The damage was done. Cesar would not be moved to change his mind, eventually causing all of the attorneys to quit en masse. By the time the dust settled, only the attorney, Diana Lyons, and I were left standing. Diana agreed to take on the appellate division. So, I had to figure out how to fill the other two division positions, Agricultural Labor Relations Board and civil litigation.

On a day following Cesar's meeting on Gavilan, I was returning to La Paz after making an appearance in San Diego Superior Court on a Union civil matter. The receptionist, Lori Huerta, relayed numerous urgent messages to me from Jerry in Los Angeles, requesting that I call him immediately. I told Lori that if he were to call again, she should tell him I was on my way back to the office and that I would call upon my arrival. But Lori insisted,

"Maybe you should call him as soon as possible. He sounds very upset."

"Okay, I'll call him."

I called from a phonebooth off the Antelope Valley Highway, in Acton, a desolate little place in the high desert where I found solace from the monotony of the long drives.

"May I speak with Jerry Cohen, please?"

Jerry got on immediately and wasted no time, flying into a tirade,

"What the fuck do you think you're doing Marco?! Do you and Cesar realize the seriousness of this shit?!"

Jerry went on rapid-fire for at least ten minutes, during which I was unable to interject anything other than sounds of feigned comprehension or acknowledgment. I had never heard Jerry so angry before, and frankly, I was concerned about him having a heart attack or stroke. At times, I would hold the phone away from my ear and look at the spring desert plants in bloom. But I heard him out.

"Okay, Jerry. I'll get back to you." He was silent before I hung up.

I drove the next forty-five minutes steeped in thought. Of course, I intended to immediately tell Cesar about the call, but pondered whether he and Jerry had stopped communicating entirely. I also wondered if the giant industry we were up against was entirely in the dark regarding the Union's schism. Upon arriving in La Paz, I immediately went to Cesar's office. He was waiting for me.

"Hi, Marco. How did it go?"

"It went well, Cesar. The case management conference was continued, which gives us more time for the discovery."

"Excellent."

"There is one other thing, however. I called Jerry from the road and he went off on a tirade."

"A tirade?" he asked.

"Yes, I can't characterize it as anything other than that."

"About what?"

"He was extremely upset about what was going down with the legal department, saying that you and I were oblivious or irresponsible concerning the 'dangers' the Union will be exposed to in various legal forums. But man, he was totally unhinged."

I waited for Cesar's response as he paused to process what I'd reported. He looked up at me from his desk.

"The son-of-a-bitch is feeling guilty."

Cesar appeared tired and upset, so I excused myself and went down to my office. It had been a long and unsettling day. Cesar gave me three warnings when I came on board the UFW: never get into a pissing contest with a skunk, never let a son-of-a-bitch know you know he's a son-of-a-bitch, and never take yourself too seriously. Those three all came to mind after our brief discussion.

In March of 1979, Cesar asked me to take over the legal department. This came as no surprise to me, but I thought it was ironic that I was being asked to replace the one other person who had influenced me to become a UFW lawyer. By then, I understood all too well to what extent the attorney-client relationship between Jerry and Cesar had deteriorated. I explained to Cesar that there was no way I could ever replace Jerry. I knew he fully understood this, but I felt it was important that I make this clear from my end. But I also assured him that given the circumstances, I was fully committed to reducing the negative impact on the Union and the ALRA that the transition could cause. We were then on the same page. He told me,

"Más hace el que quiere, que el que sabe." (He who desires to do, can do more than the one who knows how.)

By this time, it had all come to a head. After the disastrous meeting in Salinas, I knew the differences were irreconcilable, and that it would be best for all to part ways. As Cohen himself would later put it, "You want to get into an internal union political fight with Cesar Chavez, then you had better be prepared to lose."

Despite my respect for Cohen, there was never any doubt in my mind that my support could be for anyone other than Cesar. From my point of view, it was he who had been entrusted by the farmworkers to lead them. Even from a purely organizational perspective, I was of the firm opinion that the tail should never wag the dog.

There were, however, three conditions that I personally presented to Cesar before accepting the position of general counsel: that I begin receiving the regular volunteer stipend, which was now ten dollars a week, instead of the attorney amount paid me and the other attorneys in the past; that we would recruit all future legal department staff, including attorneys, as volunteers; and, that Vickie be assigned to the new legal department.

Cesar agreed to the conditions and at my request, Vickie was immediately assigned to the legal department. She was assisting Marc Grossman in New York as Cesar's East Coast advance press liaison and flew out immediately. After helping produce the "President's Newsletter" and later, the "The Wire," and assisting Ken and Gloria Doyle and Anthony Chavez prepare a FCC license application for the first UFW radio station, she would be supervising our legal staff to make sure no ALRB or court deadlines were missed.

Some years after leaving the Union, Vickie went on to law school and became a licensed California lawyer. She credits her Union experiences and Cesar's "*Si se Puede*" attitude for inspiring her.

Immediately we began to assess the lay of the land ahead of us. Our first task was to rent a large apartment in Salinas to be used by the staff during the transition. Within days we set out to Salinas with our skeleton crew. We were assisted by Larry Abrams, staff secretary to the old legal department. He and his girlfriend, Dorothy Martinez, were a great asset and committed themselves throughout the summer in guiding us through the administrative morass that was to befall us. I would be handling litigation, as well as recruiting attorneys and student volunteers in Arizona, California, and New Mexico.

While we were up to the task, the major obstacle in the transition was the negative atmosphere we encountered in the Gavilan office. While Jerry and Sandy Nathan retained a facade of civility, others in the law office went out of their way to make things difficult. Their responses to our questions were often met with curt replies and with sarcastic remarks amongst themselves. In all, there were about 400 cases transferred to us under the hostile glare of the former Salinas legal office staff. It was not the smoothest of transitions.

In a couple of months, we were packed and ready to move the law offices to La Paz. Dolores Huerta got the Bruce Church lettuce strikers to help us load the large rental U-Haul. When I met up with her outside, she said to me,

"Marco, don't give up."

"I have no intention of giving up, Dolores."

Once again, Dolores's intuition had not failed her. I was at that point so burned out that I very well may have given up had Dolores not encouraged me. I just did not dare admit my weakness.

While working in Salinas, I saw how some of the lawyers in the old legal department were even turning on each other. There were other personal reasons for this, but suffice it to say that the pressure was getting to them all, and it wasn't pretty. It was into this environment that we had come with our embryonic staff to complete the first phase of our mission — to move the new legal department to La Paz, a distance of 300 miles away. In spite of the obstacles, we succeeded.

24.

Following up on a tip from Dolores and having heard Carlos Alcala speak at Boalt Hall when I was a student there, recruiting him to join our new legal department became my number one priority. I told Cesar about him and how he would be a valuable asset in attracting other attorneys to the cause. Carlos was a Harvard Law graduate and worked under State Secretary of Health, Mario Obledo, as Chief Counsel of the Civil Rights Division, a handsomely-paid position. I had heard him lecture on civil rights at U.C. Berkeley a few years earlier and was impressed both by the impact of his litigation experience and his knowledge of the law. I told Vickie about him, and she scheduled him to appear on the community show she co-produced for KPIX, "*Sol Es Vida.*" After days of phone conversations with Carlos, I decided to act.

I told Cesar, "I'm going up to Sacramento, just packing him up, and bringing him down to La Paz." Cesar wished me luck as I left his office.

Carlos had arranged for me to meet with Mario Obledo while I was up in Sacramento. I had already heard great things about his early activist days in Texas and then later as a civil rights lawyer. Obledo co-founded the Mexican American Legal Defense and Educational Fund. He was also a co-founder of the Hispanic National Bar Association, the National Coalition of Hispanic Organizations, and an early leader of the Southwest Voter Registration Education Project. He was president of the League of United Latin American Citizens in the mid-1980s and chairman of the National Rainbow Coalition from 1988 to 1993. Through the years, Obledo had picked up the title of being the "Godfather of the Latino movement." Carlos and he were both born in San Antonio and were both proven warriors in protecting the rights of Mexican-Americans in the Southwest. After meeting him in his spacious office, I was impressed by his knowledge, but most importantly by his compassion and dedication to fighting for poor people's rights.

After our meeting, Obledo wished Carlos and I well. I believe Carlos felt better for it, leaving with the "*Don's*" blessing. I did too.

I rented a large moving truck and while Carlos was busy saying farewell to his numerous friends (as well as attending at least three going-away parties), I organized a few volunteers to help me pack his belongings. I suggested that we tow his car so that he and I could travel down in the truck together. In my mind, I had determined I would be doing the driving, lest he change his mind and turn back while en route. I had my star player and I was not about to let anyone, or anything, change his mind. The morning after the last hurrah celebration, I woke him and whispered,

"Carlos, I'll be outside in the truck," as I handed him a cup of hot coffee.

It was a beautiful morning, and I was absolutely elated as we drove south on Highway 99. Carlos was pretty spent from the last three nights of going-away parties. In between naps I would bring him up to speed about life in La Paz. He explained to me that Saturdays were his "R and R" days, and Sundays were for "kick-back".

"Absolutely," I responded, as I pulled into a gas station in Fresno. I called Cesar from a phone booth while Carlos got out and stretched. When the La Paz phone operator answered I asked for Cesar, and instead of the usual wait, he answered immediately. I coyly asked,

"Guess who I have all packed up in a U-Haul?"

"Where are you?" he responded.

"In Fresno, gassing up on our way to La Paz."

Cesar then broke into a funny John Wayne impersonation, "Bring him in, ALIVE."

Cesar and I agreed that by recruiting Carlos, my job as the new legal department head- hunter would be a lot easier. The next few months were very busy, and despite his caveat about

his weekends being for "R and R," he unflinchingly worked right through them.

Another key recruit was Marcos Camacho, who had been on the UFW picket lines with his family from a very young age. He was a junior majoring in political science at Fresno State University. I got word that he might be interested in the lawyer apprenticeship program Cesar and I had discussed as another way to demystify the law to the farmworkers. One way was the paralegal program that we had already started up. This involved people being trained in basic legal terms, law, administrative procedure, rules of evidence, and allowed to learn on the job trying cases before the ALRB.

Vickie and I went to see Marcos in the Fresno area and we told him we were recruiting staff for the new legal department, and how Diana Lyons would be supervising the appellate division, Frank Fernandez the ALRB division, and Carlos Alcala the civil litigation division. He was impressed but reiterated his educational goals in pre-law and how he planned on being a lawyer. I explained to him,

"One of Cesar's goals is to set up an apprenticeship program, so that participants, working and studying law under the supervision of a licensed attorney, can in four years qualify to take the bar exam. Tom Dalzell did that under Jerry and passed the bar on his first try, and so can you."

"Really?" he asked.

"Yes." I responded.

Marcos mulled it over for a bit. Then, smiling nervously, he said,

"Okay, but you'll need to speak with my dad first."

"Of course." I said.

Knowing Mr. Camacho was one of the Union's first supporters (and his entire family were ardent followers), made it an honor and pleasure to visit his home. Marcos introduced us and briefly filled him in on my proposal after which Mr. Camacho expressed his concerns. He emphasized that his son's plan to be a lawyer not be derailed. He looked me right in the eyes, and asked,

"Licenciado, usted me promete que mi hijo será abogado?" (*Licenciado*, do you promise me my son will be a lawyer?)

"Si Señor Camacho, se lo prometo." (Yes Mr. Camacho, I promise.)

"Ya sabe Licenciado, lo prometido es deuda." (You know *Licenciado*, a promise is a debt.)

"Así es." (So be it), I assured him, hoping it would all come through.

We shook hands and Marcos came on board. He joined two former grape-boycotters, Chris Schneider and Ned Dunphy, and the three of them later passed the California bar exam on their first try. They were supervised by our attorney, Ellen Eggers. Soon thereafter, Barbara Macri, long-time UFW volunteer, also went on to become a licensed California attorney. Eventually, they each went on to become distinguished attorneys in their own right. Marcos Camacho went on to become UFW general counsel and is now a California Superior Court judge in Kern County. Such were the first fruits of the Cesar Chavez Law School.

Cesar's eldest son, Fernando, who was an attorney, and I were introduced by a mutual friend in the early 1970s while I was visiting my family in Bakersfield. Subsequently, I would see him in San Jose when he was up seeing his grandparents, Cesar's parents. When Fernando was tried for draft evasion in Fresno federal court, he was represented pro bono by Michael Tiger, the most prominent Selective Service criminal defense attorney of the day and classmate of Jerry Cohen's at Berkeley. It was Jerry who recruited Tiger for Fernando's case, and his brilliant courtroom strategy resulted in an acquittal from the conservative, Anglo, Republican judge.

I found Fernando to be intelligent and quick-witted, with a positive disposition. When recruiting, I mentioned to Cesar that I was speaking with Fernando in the hopes that he might come on board with us. I knew it was a good idea when I saw how Cesar lit up, although I also knew that the two had their conflicts. I wrote this off to the normal stresses that can often come between father and son, especially given how demanding Cesar could be at times.

A few days later, Cesar invited me to come up with him to the Bay Area. I suggested that he drop me off at Fernando's office in San Jose so that I could have a recruitment talk with him. He agreed.

Fernando's office was on the elegant and wide street, The Alameda, which had tall trees and fashionable former homes from a gilded era, now converted to office buildings. The Chavez Law Office was in such a building, small, but quaint, and away from the busy street.

I was given a quick tour of the office by Fernando's secretary, Rosario, while Fernando finished with a couple of phone calls in what appeared to be a busy schedule. Fernando and I then relaxed a bit and I wasted no time in making my pitch. I told him about the circumstances surrounding the new legal department. Then I listed off my current roster, including Carlos Alcala whom he had heard of. Fernando listened patiently, once in a while asking me pointed but pertinent questions. He knew Cohen from the early UFW days in Delano and it was obvious he thought well of him, but he took no sides in the legal department controversy. He was sympathetic and expressed his good wishes for my endeavors, but he was quite intent on expanding his busy law practice. It all sounded exciting to me, and I understood his vision.

We said our farewells when Cesar returned to pick me up for our return trip to La Paz. As soon as I got in the car Cesar asked me how it had gone with Fernando. I explained to him it had been friendly and informative.

"So, what did he say?" Cesar asked for the bottom line.

"He said he couldn't do it."

"Did he say why? Is it his practice?"

"Yes."

Cesar paused and then said, "*Pobrecito*" (Poor guy). That was all Cesar said until we passed Gilroy, heading toward Casa de Fruta.

During the transition, some of the outgoing UFW attorneys disparaged us at every turn. There were 400 cases transferred to the new attorneys under the hostile watch of the former attorneys, two Board members, and the Salinas field office staff. They expected us to fail, and for obvious reasons, I was their main target.

It was in that spirit that I was tossed the *Stafford v. United Farmworkers* case. The court had set a firm date for jury trial. It was a personal injury case based on an accident out in the tomato fields of Yolo County. The argument was that the Union had failed to supervise the strikers who had allegedly parked partially blocking a road, which somehow led to the plaintiff substantially injuring her leg.

After sitting on this case for over four years, the old legal department handed it to me to try before a jury in the court of Judge Harry Ackley. The problems were that little, if any, discovery had been done; the plaintiff had not been examined by a defense doctor; the plaintiff's doctor had not been deposed; no accident reconstruction expert had been retained by Cohen's department; nor had the defense accident reconstruction expert been deposed.

Because of how long the case had been pending, the court refused any further continuances. I did my best contesting the plaintiff's evidence, protected the record by filing a key motion to the court, and was forced by the court to try the case. The jury awarded the plaintiff $100,000 in damages, exactly the amount stated as liquidated damages in the injunction issued by the court against the Union. When I lost the case, I called Cesar with the bad news. Cesar was momentarily silent, but then asked excitedly,

"But we can appeal, right?"

I had been so distraught from losing my first jury trial that I had forgotten all about an appeal. Cesar's question had let the sun shine through my gloomy sky!

Four years after I tried the *Stafford* case, the California Supreme Court unanimously reversed and remanded the case for trial based on the grounds that I presented at the trial, i.e. to exclude the introduction by plaintiff of the court injunction issued against the Union. Stafford's attorney had argued that the injunction was equivalent to a safety statute, which under California law, if four criteria are met, the defendant's conduct is presumed to be negligent. In the *Stafford* case, however, the Court found that one of the four criteria was not present, and that the evidence as to how the accident happened was not certain. Therefore, it ruled, that allowing the plaintiff to read from the picketing injunction, and furthermore allowing it into the jury room as evidence during deliberations, was more prejudicial than probative. For those reasons, the case was sent back to Judge Ackley for a new trial. In the best compliment the court could have paid me, the high Court's opinion stated that at the trial the plaintiff's evidence had been "hotly disputed by the Union."

On retrial the jury found in favor of the UFW.

Another civil case we inherited from Cohen's department was a libel case filed in San Francisco Superior Court, *The Garin Company v. United Farmworkers of America*. The case arose out of a Union poster depicting a six-year old girl picking onions in 100-degree heat and using a discarded pesticide container for the onions. The plaintiff, maintaining that it had been falsely accused of using child labor, filed suit against the Union demanding millions in damages. Here again, the case was handed to us soon before trial with a lot of preparation yet to do. I assigned Carlos to be lead trial counsel and he and I headed to San Francisco for what turned out to be a five-week jury trial.

At the beginning of the trial I continued with my departmental duties by phone, but once I was drawn more into the trial, I let the staff in La Paz cover for me. The attorneys representing *Garin* were from an established San Francisco firm with a long history with the plaintiff. They had conducted thorough preparation, including the deposition of Cathy Murphy, who took the photo at the center of the dispute. I had been present at the deposition taken weeks prior in Albuquerque. Cathy was very open and congenial, so as predicted she was very good on the witness stand. The main factual issue was whose field was it that the girl was working in. The company maintained it was not theirs, and we countered in the alternative, that it was either their field, or, that because of an innocent confusion of property lines and boundaries, Cathy had got it wrong; in other words, there had been no callous or reckless disregard for the truth.

After many witnesses, hundreds of exhibits, experts, and delays by the court's case calendars, the jury returned a victory for the Union, 11-1. The judge and opposing counsel were shocked by the verdict that found that the Union's allegation as to the field in question was true.

Carlos and I agreed that if the *Garin* case had been filed in Salinas rather than San Francisco, the result may have likely turned out completely different, given the animus against Cesar and the Union in Monterey County. Cesar was elated to hear the news.

At the end of 1979 we celebrated New Year's Eve in La Paz. The year had been a difficult one for our entire staff. It was also one in which we made progress with the transition to the new UFW legal department. We recruited and trained a staff of twenty full-time attorneys, paralegals, and clerical workers, most of whom were Latino, and all living in La Paz.

The legal department had been relocated from Salinas to the old La Paz guard house, which had been remodeled, carpeted, and freshly painted. Next to it was a mobile home that had also been converted to an office space. These two facilities were temporary until our permanent offices were set up in the North Unit.

We made mistakes but always analyzed and learned from them. I often told our young and inexperienced staff that we should prepare diligently, but never fear making mistakes and simply maintain a positive attitude.

One young attorney dreaded going before a particularly difficult ALRB administrative law judge, so I advised her to visualize that judge in Bermuda shorts and a Hawaiian shirt. It worked, and she laughed so hard after her next hearing that her eyes teared.

With each passing week we all increased in self-confidence and gained more experience, which allowed us to become very efficient.

After two years of the department going non-stop, we had a staff meeting. My staff was exhausted, even the "workaholics." They knew I had an upcoming meeting with Cesar and asked that I bring up the issue of vacation time. I knew how Cesar disliked the term "vacation" and so I explained that I would phrase it as "time off."

I met with Cesar in his office, one-on-one. The words "time off" sat there at the bottom of my long list of topics, waiting anxiously. Because of the tremendous workload of the department, I was hesitant to bring it up. But I owed it to my staff who had been performing magnificently. Upon mentioning the item to Cesar, he leaned back on his old wooden swivel desk chair, looked up toward the ceiling and said, "Marco, someday we'll all rest."

Two weeks later I delivered for my staff, prevailing over Cesar on the issue of "time off."

25.

Rarely does it snow in La Paz, but it was snowing the morning I told Cesar that I was moving on. It was in early February of 1981. I located him at the North Unit, warming himself by the fireplace before a board meeting. He was with Frank Ortiz, an Executive Board member and old friend of Cesar's from his Brawley days in the Imperial Valley. I had been dreading this moment. I didn't want to leave the Union so soon after taking over the legal department, but I was completely burned out from the politics. So, the reason I gave was "personal." Cesar looked at me, processed what I told him, then turned to Frank,

"You know Frank, Marco came to us just at the right time."

My departure date was set for May of 1981. Cesar tried to change my mind and asked me if there was any other job I would like to do, but I was committed to moving to Los Angeles.

Helen Chavez, Cesar's wife, dragged him to our send-off at the Memorial Day barbeque. Anytime someone decided to leave the Union, Cesar would take it personally. I was very grateful to Helen, with whom I had a very cordial relationship. My memories of her running about in La Paz with her long apron on remain among my fondest. It brought back memories of my *abuelita* in her Chihuahua *ranchito*.

The following day, as Vickie and I pulled into La Paz from having breakfast in Tehachapi, Marshall walked up to me and extended his hand.

"Hey Marco, I heard you guys were leaving. Jessica and I are leaving too, so I wanted to say goodbye."

Although I hesitated, I shook Marshall's hand. He had been hostile to us during the transition to the new legal department, but I thought, "What the heck." My mission had been accomplished. And besides,

"*Lo cortés no quita lo valiente.*" (Courtesy does not take from one's valor.)

Marc Grossman knew Cesar the last twenty-four years of his life, serving most of that time as his press secretary, speechwriter, and personal aide. As spokesperson for both the UFW and the Cesar Chavez Foundation, he has made a compilation highlighting the achievements of the UFW, as well as the Cesar Chavez Foundation, through the years.

Among the accomplishments of the UFW are: the first enduring farmworkers union; the first real union contracts in farm labor guaranteeing rest periods, toilets, clean drinking water, and hand-washing facilities in the fields; protections against pesticide poisoning (the first time that DDT was outlawed in the United States was in a UFW contract with a grape grower in 1967); the first family medical coverage, including dental and vision benefits, for farmworkers and their dependents; helping to pull the wages of many farmworkers up above the minimum wage in the state's largest agricultural regions through pressure on non-union employers from union organizing and contract gains; and so much more.

Founded under a different name in the 1960s, the Cesar Chavez Foundation is a non-profit, tax-exempt charitable organization with the mission of improving communities by preserving, promoting, and applying the legacy of Cesar Chavez. The Chavez Foundation has four core programmatic areas: 1) Housing and Economic Development Fund, which has built or renovated and manages $900 million of high-quality affordable housing in some four dozen communities in four states serving 5,000 low-income families and seniors with housing and extensive social services for youth and seniors; 2) Communications Fund, which owns and operates an 11-station educational radio network reaching 1.5 million weekly listeners and followers in four states; 3) Education Fund, which develops future leaders by providing after-school tutoring and summer session academic services for underserved students; and 4) the National Chavez Center at La Paz, Keene, CA, which preserves the legacy of Cesar and the farmworkers movement and was designated a National Park by President Barack Obama.

Cesar often stressed that these accomplishments were made possible by the labors of thousands of volunteers in the movement. It is a great legacy of which all UFW staffers and supporters can be proud of.

Despite these accomplishments, however, the present condition in the fields is dismal. It has been estimated that less than one percent of farmworkers enjoy the protections of collective bargaining. Also, there are estimates that over fifty percent of the agricultural labor force is undocumented, coming principally from deep in Mexico and increasingly indigenous peoples (Mixtecos, Zapotecas, Triqui, and others). They are suspicious of any governmental agency. When one adds to this the fact that the Agricultural Labor Relations Board has been politically emasculated, it becomes evident why this work force is once again extremely vulnerable.

Cesar's life was shortened by years of struggle, sacrifice, and constant travels. He dedicated himself entirely to the cause of farmworkers. He was only sixty-six when he passed away in his native Arizona, spent but unbent.

Two months before he died on April 23, 1993, Cesar called me at my law office in San Diego. He was excited to tell me that he had plans for a project in Mexico. He didn't give any details, nor did I ask. We had not spoken in over three years, and it was good to hear his voice.

"But why call me?" I thought.

Cesar asked me if he could count on me to find him a good Mexican lawyer.

"An honest one though, okay?" he added.

"Of course," I responded.

We agreed to talk soon, but it would be the last time he and I spoke.

It had been twelve long years since I had left the UFW, and so I was happy to have Dolores as our guest whenever she was doing contract negotiations in the San Diego area. It was always great getting the latest Union news and to hear about our old friends from the UFW. One morning when Dolores was staying with us, she came downstairs while I was making breakfast and excitedly asked,

"Guess what I dreamed about last night?"

I was stumped, so I looked at her and asked,

"What did you dream about?"

She was glowing as she described how in her dream she was staying at our house, but in the dream, our house was in La Paz. She continued,

"I walked outside, and it was a beautiful day! The sun was up, the many flowers vibrant, as was the creek that was flowing full and sparkling. I saw Cesar on the other side of the creek and called to him, but it was as if he didn't hear me—he didn't respond."

Dolores gave me one of her probing, quizzical looks.

"It's his birthday today. Let's call him and wish him a happy birthday!"

"Yeah!" Vickie and I exclaimed simultaneously.

I handed Dolores the phone. Dolores called but there was no answer. We knew that the Founders' Day celebrations in La Paz had likely begun; the singing of *Las Mañanitas* to Cesar from outside his bedroom window, the coffee and hot chocolate with *pan dulce* enjoyed in the community kitchen, and then the party in the North Unit. Those had been very happy days in La Paz, and we three shared how we wished we were there with him.

*

* * * *

*

*

Cesar Chavez's mother and father, Juana Estrada and Librado Chavez, were both born in the state of Chihuahua, Mexico. He had Rarámuri, or Tarahumara blood as the Spaniards referred to them. Cesar was therefore a first-generation Mexican-American since he, himself, had been born in Yuma, Arizona in 1927. Shortly before Cesar's death, he and his younger brother Richard traveled to their parents' home-state of Chihuahua to investigate their family roots and the Tarahumara of the Sierra Madre Occidental. I do not know what Cesar and Richard's impressions were of that trip. I have wondered if they made the trip by train to the Copper Canyon. If so, I suspect that they too were captivated by its noble people, the magnificent canyons four times the size of the Grand Canyon, the colorful clothes and dances, the delicious traditional dishes, and their nature-based religion that honors Mother Earth who provides them with beans and corn. They are people who isolated themselves from the Spaniards, as well as from the Mexicans, whom they view as dishonest and greedy. The Tarahumara believe that wealth cannot make one happy, but rather, happiness is the result of being content with the basic necessities of life.

Hearing about their trip took me back to those remarkable days in 1958, with the scent of pinewood rising from the chimney tops into the crisp cold air, the smell of corn tortillas on my *abuelita's* wood-burning stove, and *tío* Mike, spinning us a *cuento* of a pilgrimage north.

Sierra de Quesada

En la sierra de Quesada
hay un águila gigante,
verdosa, negra y dorada,
siempre las alas abiertas.
Es de piedra y no se cansa.
Pasado Puerto Lorente,
entre las nubes galopa,
el caballo de los montes.
Nunca se cansa: es de roca.
En el hondón del barranco
se ve al jinete caído,
que alza los brazos al cielo.
Los brazos son de granito.
Y allí donde nadie sube
hay una virgen risueña
con un río azul en brazos.
Es la virgen de la sierra.

~Por Antonio Machado

CPSIA information can be obtained
at www.ICGtesting.com
Printed in the USA
FSHW021958040621
82114FS

9 781889 568010